Teacher Certification Exam

Special Education Volume 2
Emotionally Handicapped

Written By:

Kathy Schnirman, PhD. Special Education

To Order Additional Copies:
Xam, Inc.
99 Central St.
Worcester, MA 01605
Toll Free   1-800-301-4647
Phone: 1-508 363 0633
Email: winwin1111@aol.com
Web   www.xamonline.com
EFax   1-501-325-0185
Fax: 1-508-363-0634

You will find:
- Content Review in prose format
- Bibliography
- Sample Test

XAM, INC.
Building Better Teachers

"And, while there's no reason yet to panic, I think it's only prudent that we make preperations to panic."

Printed in the United States of America

MTTC: Special Education Volume 2 Emotionally Handicapped
ISBN: 1-58197-209-1

COMPETENCY 1.0   KNOWLEDGE OF FOUNDATIONS

Skill 1. 1   Identify federal legislation pertaining to exceptional students.

Background. The U. S. Constitution does not specify protection for education. However, all states provide education, and thus individuals are guaranteed protection and due process under the 14th Amendment. The basic source of law for special education is the Individuals with Disabilities Education Act (IDEA) and its accompanying regulations.   IDEA represents the latest phase in the philosophy of educating children with disabilities.   Initially, children with disabilities often did not go to school. When they did, they were segregated into special classes in order to avoid disrupting the regular class. Their education usually consisted of simple academics and later training for manual jobs.

By the mid-1900s, advocates for handicapped children argued that segregation was inherently unequal. By the time of P. L. 94-142, about half of the estimated 8 million handicapped children in the U. S. were either not being appropriately served in school or were excluded from schooling altogether.   There was a disproportionate number of minority children placed in special programs. Identification and placement practices and procedures were inconsistent, and parental involvement was generally not encouraged. After segregation on the basis of race was declared unconstitutional in Brown v. Board of Education, parents and other advocates filed similar lawsuits on behalf of children with handicaps. The culmination of their efforts resulted in P. L. 94-142. This section is a brief summary of that law and other major legislation which affect the manner in which special education services are delivered to handicapped children.

Supreme Court Cases Significant to the Development of P. L. 94-142

1. Brown v. Board of Education, 1954. While this case specifically addressed the inequality of "separate but equal" facilities on the basis of race, the concept that segregation was inherently unequal—even if equal facilities were provided—was later applied to handicapping conditions.

2. Pennsylvania Association for Retarded Citizens (PARC) v. Commonwealth of Pennsylvania, 1972. Special education was guaranteed to children with mental retardation. The victory in this case sparked other court cases for children with other disabilities.

3. Mills v. Board of Education of the District of Columbia, 1972. The right to special education was extended to all children with disabilities, not just mentally retarded children. Judgements in PARC and Mills paved the way for P. L. 94-142.

Significant Legislation With an Impact on Exceptional Student Education

I. Section 504, Rehabilitation Act of 1973. Section 504 expands an older law by extending its protection from employment to other areas that receive federal assistance, such as education. Protected individuals must (a) have a physical or mental impairment that substantially limit one or more major life activities, such as self-care, walking, seeing, breathing, working, and learning. (b) have a record of such an impairment, or (c) be regarded as having such an impairment. A disability in itself is not sufficient grounds for a complaint of discrimination. The person must be otherwise qualified, or able to meet, the requirements of the program in question.

II. Americans with Disabilities Act (ADA) 1990. Bars discrimination in employment, transportation, public accommodations, and telecommunications in all aspects of life, not just those receiving federal funding. Title II and Title III are applicable to special education because they cover the private sector (such as private schools) and require access to public accommodations. New and remodeled public buildings, transportation vehicles, and telephone systems now must be accessible to the handicapped. ADA also protects individuals with contagious diseases, such as AIDS, from discrimination.

III. P. L. 94-142 (Education for All Handicapped Children Act)--1975. The philosophy behind these pieces of legislation is that education is to be provided to **all** children (6-18) who meet age eligibility requirements. All children are assumed to be capable of benefiting from education. For children with severe or profound handicaps, "education" may be interpreted to include training in basic self-help skills and vocational training as well as academics.

The principles of IDEA also incorporate the concept of "normalization". Within this concept, persons with disabilities are allowed access to everyday patterns and conditions of life that are as close as possible or equal to their nondisabled peers. There are 7 fundamental provisions of IDEA:

1. Free appropriate public education (FAPE). Special education services are to be provided at no cost to students or their families. The federal and state governments share any additional costs. FAPE also requires that education be appropriate to the individual needs of the students.

2. Notification and procedural rights for parents. These include:

* Right to examine records and obtain independent evaluations

* Right to receive a clearly written notice that states the results of the school's evaluation of their child and whether the child meets eligibility requirements for placement or continuation of special services

* Parents who disagree with the school's decision may request a **due process** hearing and a **judicial hearing** if they do not receive satisfaction through due process.

3. _Identification and services to all children_: States must conduct public outreach programs to seek out and identify children who may need services.

4. _Necessary related services_: Developmental, corrective, and other support services that make it possible for a student to benefit from special education services must be provided. These may include speech, recreation, or physical therapy.

5. _Individualized assessments_: Evaluations and tests must be nondiscriminatory and individualized.

6. _Individualized Education Plans (IEP)_: Each student receiving special education services must have an individualized education plan developed at a meeting that is attended by a qualified representative of the local education agency (LEA). Others who should attend would be the proposed special education teachers, mainstream teachers, parents, and--when appropriate--the student.

7. _Least Restrictive Environment (LRE)_: There is no simple definition of LRE. LRE differs with the individual child's needs. LRE means that the student is placed in an environment which is not dangerous or overly controlling or intrusive. The student should be given opportunities to experience what other peers of similar mental or chronological age are doing. Finally, LRE should be the environment which is the most integrated and normalized for the student's strengths and weaknesses. LRE for one child may be a regular classroom with support services, while LRE for another may be a self-contained classroom in a special school.

IV. **P. L. 99-457 (1986).** Beginning with the 1991-92 school year, special education programs were required for children ages 3 to 5, with most states offering outreach programs to identify children with special needs from birth to age 3. In place of or in addition to an annual IEP, the entire family's needs are addressed by an Individual Family Service Plan (IFSP), which is reviewed with the family every 6 months.

necessary academic and/or vocational preparation during high school. Interagency participation in the transition plan can help the student and family in identifying needs and sources of assistance to facilitate the transition to the demands of adult living, when public school support is no longer available. Finally, the school can serve as the coordinator of services and agencies while the student is still in school

Significant Supreme Court Cases Involving Interpretation of IDEA

Following the passage of P. L. 94-142 and IDEA, questions have arisen over the interpretation of the concepts of "least restrictive environment" and "free, appropriate public education". The courts have been asked to judge the extent of a school district's obligation to provide "support services" and suspension procedures for students with disabilities. A brief description of some of the cases that were reviewed by the U. S. Supreme Court and the rulings is included in this section. These cases have included issues such as least restrictive environment, free and appropriate public education, transportation, suspension of exceptional education students, and provision of services in a private school setting.

Board of Education v. Rowley, 1982. Amy Rowley was a deaf elementary school student whose parents rejected their school district's proposal to provide a tutor and speech therapist services to supplement their daughter's instruction in the regular classroom. Her parents insisted on an interpreter, even though Amy was making satisfactory social, academic, and educational progress without one. In deciding in favor of the school district, the Supreme Court ruled that school districts must provide those services that permit a student with disabilities to benefit from instruction. Essentially, the court ruled that the states are obligated to provide a "basic floor of opportunity" that is reasonable to allow the child to benefit from special education.

Irving Independent School District v. Tatro, 1984. IDEA lists health services as one of the "related services" that schools are mandated to provide to exceptional students. Amber Tatro, who had spina bifida, required the insertion of a catheter on a regular schedule in order to empty her bladder. The issue was specifically over the classification of clean intermittent catheterization (CIC) as a medical service (not covered under IDEA) or a "related health service", which would be covered. In this instance, the cathetherization was not declared a medical service, but a "related service" necessary for the student to have in order to benefit from special education. The school district was obliged to provide the service. The Tatro case has implications for students with other medical impairments who may need services to allow them to attend classes at the school.

Smith v. Robinson. This 1984 case concerned reimbursement of attorney's fees for parents who win litigation under IDEA. At the time of this case IDEA did not provide for such reimbursement. Following this ruling, Congress passed a law awarding attorney's fees to parents who win their litigation.

Honig v. Doe, 1988. Essentially, students may not be denied education or exclusion from school when their misbehavior is related to their handicap. The "stay put" provision of IDEA allows students to remain in their current educational setting pending the outcome of administrative or judicial hearings. In the case of behavior which is a danger to the student or others, the court allows school districts to apply their normal procedures for dealing with dangerous behavior, such as time-out, loss of privileges, detention, or study carrels.. Where the student has presented an immediate threat to others, that student may be temporarily suspended for up to 10 school days to give the school and the parents time to review the IEP and discuss possible alternatives to the current placement.

Skill 1.2   Recognize the continuum of services available in exceptional student education.

In order to comply with the principle of individualized education in the lease restrictive environment (LRE), schools have developed a continuum of delivery models to meet students' needs. This continuum is sometimes referred to as an "array of services". One well-known depiction of this continuum is Deno's Cascade of Services, in which the continuum of services is represented as a triangle. In this model, the number of students requiring more restrictive services decreases as the degree of restrictiveness increases. The expenses involved in providing services also increase with the degree of restrictivness as well. The idea of a continuum of services also implies that a student is not "locked" into a particular program or setting. The student can move to more or less restrictive placements along this continuum of services according to changes in his or needs and ability to function within a particular placement.

The following table represents the types of services on the continuum, beginning with the least restrictive and ending with the most restrictive.

LOCATION OF SERVICE	DESCRIPTION
Regular classroom	Student functions in the regular classroom with no special assistance or services
Itinerant teacher or Consultation in Regular Classroom	Student receives consultation or assistance from a special education teacher who comes to the classroom.
Resource room	Student remains in the regular classroom most of the time, but goes to a special education class for certain subjects or blocks of time.
Partially self-contained special education class	Student attends some regular education classes and some special education classes, depending on the IEP
Self-contained special education class	Minimal attendance in regular education classes; majority of time spent in special education classes
Center school	Student attends a school designed to service a specific type of disability. May or may not be located in the student's neighborhood. May or may not be residential. May be a public school or a private school supported by the state.
Other placements outside the school setting	Includes residential hospital (i.e., psychiatric or substance abuse) facilities, homebound placement, and services in juvenile correctional facilities or programs.

COMPETENCY 2.0 UNDERSTANDING OF DEFINITIONS, CHARACTERISTICS, AND TERMINOLOGY

Skill 2.1 Explain the definitions and classification systems in exceptional student education.

IDEA defines handicapped children as children "evaluated in accordance with 300.530-300.534 as being mentally retarded, hard of hearing, deaf, speech impaired, visually handicapped, seriously emotionally disturbed, orthopedically impaired, other health impaired, deaf-blind, multi-handicapped, or as having specific learning disabilities, who because of those impairments need special education and related services (300.5).. Having these conditions does not in itself qualify a child as handicapped under this law. The condition must prevent a child from being able to benefit from education.

The classification of exceptional student education is a categorical system, since it organizes special education into categories. Within the categories are subdivisions which may be based on the severity or level of support services needed. Having a categorical system allows educators to differentiate and define types of disabilities, relate treatments to certain categories, and concentrate research and advocacy efforts. The disadvantage of the categorical system is the labeling of groups or individuals. Critics of labels say that labeling can place the emphasis of the label and not the individual needs of the child. The following table summarizes the categories of handicapping conditions and major characteristics of their definitions.

Classifications of Handicapping Conditions Under IDEA

Classification	Characteristics
Deaf	Impairment in processing linguistic information with or without hearing aids that adversely impacts educational performance
Deaf-blind	Hearing and visual impairments causing communication, developmental, and educational problems too severe to be met in programs solely for deaf or blind children
Hard of hearing	Permanent or fluctuating hearing impairment that adversely affects educational performance, but is not

	included in the definition of deafness
Mentally retarded	Significantly subaverage general intellectual functioning with deficits in adaptive behavior, manifested during the developmental period, and adversely affecting educational performance
Multihandicapped	Combination of impairments, excluding deaf-blind children, which causes educational problems too severe to be serviced in programs designed for a single impairment
Orthopedically impaired	Severe orthopedic impairment adversely affecting educational performance, resulting from birth defects, disease (e.g., polio), or other causes (e.g., amputation, burns)
Other health impaired	Autism and medical conditions such as heart conditions, tuberculosis, rheumatic fever, nephritis, asthma, sickle cell anemia, hemophilia, epilepsy, lead poisoning, leukemia, or diabetes. (IDEA listing). Other health conditions may be included if they are so chronic or acute that the child's strength, vitality, or alertness is limited.
Seriously emotionally disturbed (Does not include children who are socially maladjusted unless they are also classified seriously emotionally disturbed.)	Schizophrenia, and conditions in which 1 or more of these characteristics is exhibited over a long period of time and to a marked degree: (a) inability to learn not explained by intellectual, sensory, or health factors, (b) inability to build or maintain satisfactory interpersonal relationships, (c) inappropriate types of behavior or feelings, (d) general pervasive unhappiness or depression, (e) tendency to develop physical symptoms or fears associated with personal or school problems

Specific learning disability	Disorder in 1 or more basic psychological processes involved in understanding or in using spoken or written language, which manifests itself in an imperfect ability to listen, think, speak, read, write, spell, or do mathematical calculations. They cannot be attributed to visual, hearing, physical, intellectual, or emotional handicaps, or cultural, environmental, or economic disadvantage.
Speech impaired	Communication disorder such as stuttering, impaired articulation, voice impairment, or language impairment adversely affecting educational performance.
Visually handicapped (Partially sighted or blind)	Visual impairment, even with correction, adversely affecting educational performance.

It should be noted that there is no classification for gifted children under IDEA. Funding and services for gifted programs are left up to the individual states and school districts. Therefore, the number of districts providing services and the scope of gifted programs varies among states and school districts.

Skill 2.2 Explain the definitions and classification systems of emotionally handicapped children.

Children whose behavior deviates from society's standards for normal behavior for certain ages and stages of development. Behavioral expectations vary from setting to setting—for example, it is acceptable to yell on the football field, but not as the teacher is explaining a lesson to the class. Different cultures have their standards of behavior, further complicating the question of what constitutes a behavioral problem. People also have their personal opinions and standards for what is tolerable and what is not. Some behavioral problems are openly expressed; others are inwardly directed and not very obvious. As a result of these factors, the terms behavioral disorders and emotional disturbance have become almost interchangeable.

While almost all children at times exhibit behaviors that are aggressive, withdrawn, or otherwise inappropriate, the IDEA definition of serious emotional disturbance focuses on behaviors that persist over time, intense, and impair a child's ability to function in society. The behaviors must not be caused by temporary stressful situations or other causes (i.e., depression over the death of a grandparent, or anger over the parents' impending divorce). In order for a child to be considered seriously emotionally disturbed, he or she must exhibit one or more of the following characteristics over a **long period of time** and to a **marked degree** that **adversely affects** a child's educational performance:

- Inability to learn that cannot be explained by intellectual, sensory, or health factors
- Inability to build or maintain satisfactory interpersonal relationships
- Inappropriate types of behaviors or feelings under normal conditions
- General pervasive mood of unhappiness or depression
- Physical symptoms or fears associated with personal or school problems.
- Schizophrenic children are covered under this definition, and social maladjustment by itself does not satisfy this definition unless it is accompanied by one of the other conditions of SED.

The diagnostic categories and definitions used to classify mental disorders come from the American Psychiatric Association's publication Diagnostic and Statistical Manual of Mental Disorders (DSM-III), the handbook which is used by psychiatrists and psychologists. The DSM-III is a multiaxial classification system consisting of dimensions (axes) coded along with the psychiatric diagnosis. The axes are:

- *Axis I*: Principal psychiatric diagnosis (e.g.,Overanxious disorder)
- *Axis II:* Developmental problems (e.g., developmental reading disorder
- *Axis III*--Physical disorders (e.g., allergies)
- *Axis IV*--Psychosocial stressors (e.g., divorce)
- *Axis V*--Rating of the highest level of adaptive functioning (includes intellectual and social). Rating is called Global Assessment Functioning (GAF) score.

While the DSM-III diagnosis is one way of diagnosing serious emotional disturbance, there are other ways of classifying the various forms that behavior disorders manifest themselves. The following tables summarize some of these classifications.

Externalizing Behaviors	Internalizing Behaviors
Aggressive behaviors expressed outwardly toward others.	Withdrawing behaviors that are directed inward to oneself
Manifested as hyperactivity, persistent aggression, irritating behaviors that are impulsive and distractible	Social withdrawal
Examples: Hitting, cursing, stealing,	Depression, fears, phobias, elective

arson, cruelty to animals, hyperactivity, theft	mutism, withdrawal, anorexia and bulimia		

Well-known instruments used to assess children's behavior have their own categories (scales) to classify behaviors. The following table illustrates the scales used in some of the widely-used instruments:

Walker Problem Identification Checklist	Burks' Behavior Rating Scales (BBRS)	Devereux Behavior Rating Scale (Adolescent)	Revised Behavior Problem Checklist (Quay & Peterson)
Acting out	Excessive self-blame	Unethical behavior	Major Scales
Withdrawal	Excessive anxiety	Defiant-resistive	Conduct Disorder
Distractibility	Excessive withdrawal	Domineering-sadistic	Socialized aggression
Disturbed peer Relations	Excessive dependency	Heterosexual interest	Attention-problems--immaturity
Immaturity	Poor ego strength	Hyperactive expansive	Anxiety-Withdrawal
	Poor physical strength	Poor emotional control	
	Poor coordination	Need approval, dependency	Minor Scales
	Poor intellectuality	Emotional disturbance	Psychotic behavior
	Poor academics	Physical inferiority-timidity	Motor excess
	Poor attention	Schizoid withdrawal	
	Poor impulse control	Bizarre speech and cognition	
	Poor reality contact	Bizarre actions	
	Poor sense of identify		
	Excessive suffering		
	Poor anger control		
	Excessive sense of persecution		
	Excessive aggressiveness		
	Excessive resistance		
	Poor social		

	conformity		

Disturbance may also be categorized in degrees: mild, moderate, or severe. The degree of disturbance will affect the type and degree of interventions and services required by emotionally handicapped students. Degree of disturbance also must be considered when determining the least restrictive environment and the services needed for free, appropriate education for these students. An example of a set of criteria for determining the degree of disturbance is the one developed by P. L. Newcomer:

	DEGREE	OF	DISTURBANCE
CRITERIA	Mild	Moderate	Severe
Precipitating events	Highly stressful	Moderately stressful	Not stressful
Destructiveness	Not destructive	Occasionally destructive	Usually destruction
Maturational appropriateness	Behavior typical for age	Some behavior untypical for age	Behavior too young or too old
Personal functioning	Cares for own needs	Usually cares for own needs	Unable to care for own needs
Social functioning	Usually able to relate to others	Usually unable to relate to others	Unable to relate to others
Reality index	Usually sees events as they are	Occasionally sees events as they are	Little contact with reality
Insight index	Aware of behavior	Usually aware of behavior	Usually not aware of behavior
Conscious control	Usually can control behavior	Occasionally can control behavior	Little control over behavior
Social responsiveness	Usually acts appropriately	Occasionally acts appropriately	Rarely acts appropriately

Source: *Understanding and Teaching Emotionally Disturbed Children and Adolescents*, (2nd ed., p. 139), by P. L. Newcomer, 1993, Austin, TX: Pro-Ed. Copyright 1993. Reprinted with permission.

Skill 2.3 Identify characteristics of normal child development.

Normality in child behavior is influenced by society's attitudes and cultural beliefs about what is normal for children. (e.g., The motto for the Victorian era was

"Children should be seen and not hears.". However, criteria for what is "normal" involves consideration of these questions
:

- *Is the behavior age-appropriate?.* An occasional tantrum may be expected for a toddler, but is not typical of a high school student.
- *Is the behavior pathological in itself?* Drug or alcohol use would be harmful to children, regardless of how many engage in it.
- *How persistent is the problem?* A kindergarten student initially may be afraid to go to school. However, if the fear persisted into first or second grade, then the problem would be considered persistent.
- *How severe is the behavior?*--Self-injurious, cruel, and extremely destructive behaviors, would be examples of behaviors that require intervention.
- *How often does the behavior occur?*--An occasional tantrum in a young child or a brief mood of depression in an adolescent would not be considered problematic. However, if the behaviors occur frequently, that behavior would not be characteristic of normal child development.
- *Do several problem behaviors occur as a group?*--Clusters of behaviors, especially severe behaviors, that occur together may be indicative of a serious problem, such as schizophrenia.
- *Is the behavior sex-appropriate?* Cultural and societal attitudes toward gender change over time. While attitudes toward younger boys playing with dolls or girls preferring sports to dolls have relaxed, children eventually are expected as adults to conform to the expected behaviors for males and females.

Certain stages of child development have their own sets of problems, and it should be kept in mind that short-term undesirable behaviors can and will occur over these stages. Child development is also a continuum, and children may manifest these problem behaviors somewhat earlier or later than their peers.

Problem Behaviors Associated with Childhood Stages of Development
(See Gelfand et al., p.120)

Toddler (1-3)	Preschool (3-5)`	Elementary (6-10)	Early Adolescence	Adolescent 15-18
Temper Tantrums	Temper Tantrums	Temper Tantrums	Temper Tantrums	--
Refuses to do things when asked	Refusal to do things when asked	--	-	-
Demands constant attention	Demands constant attention	--	--	--

13

Overactivity	Overactivity	Overactivity	--	--
Specific fears	Specific Fears	--	--	--
--	Over-Sensitivity	Over Sensitivity	Oversensitivity	--
Inattentive	--	--	--	--
--	Lying	Lying	--	--
--	--	Jealousy	Jealousy	--
--	Negativism	--	--	--
		School achievement problems	School Achievement Problems	School Achievement Problems
--	--	Excessive reserve	Excessive Reserve	--
--	--	--	Moodiness	--
--	--	--	--	Substance Abuse
--	--	--	--	Truancy or Skipping School
--	--	--	--	Minor law violations (i.e.,stealing, trespassing)
--	--	--	--	Sexual misconduct

Skill 2.4 Identify the physical, psychological, educational, and behavioral characteristics of exceptional students.

About 10% of the school-aged population between 6 and 17 years old receive special education services. Most of these exceptional students are considered mildly handicapped. The categories of mental handicaps, learning disabilities, and emotional disturbance are the three most prevalent. Exceptional students are very much like their peers without handicaps. The main difference is that they have an intellectual, emotional, behavioral, or physical deficit that significantly interferes with their ability to benefit from education.

Skill 2.5 Identify the characteristics of emotionally handicapped children.

Children with emotional handicaps or behavioral disorders are not always easy to identify. It is, of course, easy to identify the acting-out child who is constantly fighting, who cannot stay on task for more than a few minutes, or who shouts obscenities when angry. It is not always easy to identify the child who internalizes his or her problems, on the other hand, may appear to be the "model" student, but suffers from depression, shyness, or fears. Unless the problem becomes severe enough to impact school performance, the internalizing child may go for a long periods without being identified or served.

Studies of children with behavioral and emotional disorders, share some general characteristics:

Lower academic performance. While it is true that some emotionally disturbed children have above-average IQ scores, the majority are behind their peers in measures of intelligence and school achievement. Most score in the "slow learner" or "mildly mentally retarded" range on IQ tests, averaging about 90. Many have learning problems that exacerbate their acting-out or "giving-up" behavior. Adding to the achievement problem is the valuable class time lost while the child was engaged in the disruptive behavior. As the child enters secondary school, the gap between him or her and nonhandicapped peers widens until the child may be as many as 2 to 4 years behind in reading and/or math skills by high school. Children with severe degrees of impairment may be untestable at all.

Social skill deficits. Students with deficits may be uncooperative, selfish in dealings with others, unaware of what to do in social situations, or ignorant of the consequences of their actions. This may be a combination of lack of prior training, lack of opportunities to interact, and dysfunctional value systems and beliefs learned from their family.

Classroom Behaviors: Often classroom behavior is highly disruptive to the classroom setting. Emotionally disturbed children often are out of their seat or running around the room, hitting, fighting, or disturbing their classmates, stealing or destroying property, defiant and noncompliance, and/or verbally disruptive. They do not follow directions and often do not complete assignments.

Aggressive Behaviors: Aggressive children often fight or instigate their peers to strike back at them. Aggressiveness may also take the form of vandalism or destruction of property. Aggressive children also engage in verbal abuse.

Delinquency: As emotionally disturbed, acting-out children enter adolescence, they may become involved in socialized aggression (i.e., gang membership) and delinquency. Delinquency is a legal definition rather than a medical, and describes truancy and crimes that would also be illegal if they were committed by adults. Of course, not every delinquent is classified as emotionally disturbed, but children with behavioral and emotional disorders are especially at risk for becoming delinquent because of their problems at school (the primary place for socializing with peers), deficits in social skills that may make them unpopular at school, and/or dysfunctional homes.

15

Withdrawn Behaviors: Children who manifest withdrawn behaviors may consistently act in an immature fashion or prefer younger children to play with. They may daydream, complain or being sick in order to "escape" to the clinic, cry, cling to the teacher, ignore others' attempts to interact, or suffer from fears or depression.

Schizophrenic and Psychotic children may have bizarre delusions, hallucinations, incoherent thoughts, and disconnected thinking. Schizophrenia typically manifests itself between the ages of 15 and 45, and the younger the onset, the more severe the disorder. These behaviors usually require intensive treatment beyond the scope of the regular classroom setting.

Autism. Autism appears very early in childhood. The disorder is associated with brain damage and sever language impairment. Six common features of autism are:

* Apparent sensory deficit--The child may appear not to see or hear or react to a stimulus, then react in an extreme fashion to a seemingly insignificant stimulus.
* Severe affect isolation --The child does not respond to the usual signs of affection such as smiles and hugs.
* Self-stimulation--Stereotyped behavior takes the form of repeated or ritualistic actions that make no sense to others, such as hand flapping, rocking, staring at objects, humming the same sounds for hours at a time.
* Tantrums and Self-Injurious Behavior (SIB)--Autistic children may bite themselves, pull their hair, bang their heads, or hit themselves. They can throw severe tantrums and direct aggression and destructive behavior toward others.
* Echolalia --Also known as "parrot talk", the autistic child may repeat what they hear on television, for example, or respond to others by repeating what was said to them. Alternatively, they may simply not talk at all.
* Severe deficits in behavior and self-care skills--Autistic children may behave like children much younger than themselves.

Gender: Many more boys than girls are identified as having emotional and behavior problems, especially hyperactivity and attention-deficit disorder, autism, childhood psychosis, and problems with undercontrol (aggression, socialized aggression). Girls, on the other hand, have more problems with overcontrol (i.e., withdrawal and phobias). Boys also are much more prevalent than girls in numbers of children with mental retardation. and language and learning disabilities.

Age Characteristics: Identification of behavior disorders begins to increase and peak during the middle grades, and decline starting in middle school. When they enter adolescence, girls tend to experience affective or emotional disorders such as anorexia, depression, bulimia, and anxiety at twice the rate as the boys, which mirrors the adult prevalence pattern. Boys continue to dominate the numbers of disorders involving antisocial behavior and aggression.

* *Family Characteristics*: Having a child with an emotional or behavioral disorder does not automatically mean that the family is dysfunctional. However, there are family factors that create or contribute to the development and degree of behavior disorders and emotional disturbance.
* Abuse and neglect
* Lack of appropriate supervision
* Lax, punitive, and/or lack of discipline
* High rates of negative types of interaction among family members
* Lack of parental concern and interest
* Negative adult role models
* Lack of proper health care and/or nutrition
* Disruption in the family

COMPETENCY 3. PROFICIENCY IN ASSESSMENT AND EVALUATION

Skill 3.1 Identify the purposes of evaluation.

Assessment is the gathering of information in order to make decisions. In exceptional student education, assessment is used to make decisions about:

- Screening and initial identification of children who may need services
- Selection and evaluation of teaching strategies and programs
- Determination of the child's present level of performance
- Classification and program placement
- Development of goals, objectives, and evaluation for the IEP
- Eligibility for a program
- Continuation in a program
- Effectiveness of instructional programs and strategies
- Effectiveness of behavioral interventions

Skill 3. 2 Define measurement terminology.

COMMONLY ENCOUNTERED TERMS IN TESTING AND OBSERVATIONS

The following terms are frequently used in behavioral as well as academic testing and assessment. They represent basic terminology and not more advanced statistical concepts.

Baseline--Also known as establishing a baseline, this procedure means collecting data about a target behavior or performance of a skill before certain interventions or teaching procedures are implemented. Establishing a baseline will enable a person to determine if the interventions are effective.

Criterion-Referenced Test--A test in which the individual's performance is measured against mastery of curriculum criteria rather than comparison to the performance of other students. Criterion-referenced tests may be commercially or teacher-made. Since these tests measure what a student can or cannot do, results are especially use for identifying goals and objectives for IEPs and lesson plans.

Curriculum-Based Assessment--Assessment of an individual's performance of objectives of a curriculum, such as a reading or math program. The individual's performance is measured in terms of what objectives were mastered.

Duration recording--measuring the length of time a behavior lasts, i.e., tantrums, time out of class, or crying

Error Analysis--The mistakes on an individual's test are noted and categorized by type. For example, an error analysis in a reading test could categorize mistakes by miscues, substituting words, omitted words or phrases, and miscues that are self-corrected.

Event recording--The number of time a target behavior occurs during an observation period.

Formal Assessment--Standardized tests that have specific procedures for administration, norming, scoring, and interpretation. These include intelligence and achievement tests.

Frequency--the number of times a behavior occurs in a time interval, such as out-of-seat behavior, hitting, tantrums.

Frequency Distribution--Plotting the scores received on a test and tallying how many individuals received those scores. A frequency distribution is used to visually determine how the group of individuals performed on a test, illustrate extreme scores, and compare the distribution to the mean or other criterion.

Informal Assessment--Nonstandardized tests such as criterion-referenced tests and teacher-prepared tests. There are no rigid rules or procedures for administration or scoring.

Intensity--The degree of a behavior as measured by its frequency and duration.

Interval recording--This technique involves breaking the observation period into an equal number of time intervals, such as 10-second intervals during a 5-minute period. At the end of each interval, the observer notes the presence or absence of the target behavior. The observer can then calculate a percentage by dividing the number of intervals in which the target behavior occurred by the total number of intervals in the observation period. This type of recording works well for behaviors which occur with high frequency or for long periods of time, such as on- or off-task behavior, pencil tapping, or stereotyped behaviors. The observer does not have to constantly monitor the student, yet can gather enough data to get an accurate idea of the extent of the behavior.

Latency--the length of time that elapses between the presentation of a stimulus (e.g., a question) and the response (e.g., the student's answer).

Mean--The arithmetic average of a set of scores, calculated by adding up the scores and dividing the sum by the total number of scores. For example, if the total sum of a set of 35 scores was 2935, dividing that sum by 35 (the number of scores received) would yield a mean of 83.8%.

Median--The middle score at which 50% of the scores are above and 50% are below . In the example above, the middle score might be 72 . In this case, half of the 35 scores fell below 72 and the other half scored above 72.

Mode--The score most frequently tallied in a frequency distribution. In the example above, the most frequently tallied score might be 78. It is possible for a test to have more than one mode.

Momentary time sampling--Technique used for measuring behaviors of a group of individuals or several behaviors from the same individual. Time samples are usually brief, and may be conducted at fixed or variable intervals. The advantage of using variable intervals is increased reliability, since the students will not be able to predict when the time sample will be taken.

Multiple Baseline Design--May be used to test the effectiveness of an intervention in a skill performance or to determine if the intervention accounted for observed changes in a target behavior. First, the initial baseline data is collected, followed by data during the intervention period. To get the second baseline, the intervention is removed for a period of time and data is collected again. Then the intervention is re-applied and data collected on the target behavior.

An example of a multiple baseline design might be ignoring a child who calls out in class without raising his hand. Initially, the baseline could involve counting the number of times that the child calls out before applying interventions. During the time the teacher ignores the child's call-outs, data is collected. The child's call-outs would probably decrease during this time. For the second baseline, the teacher would resume the response to the child's call-outs in the way she did before ignoring. The child's call-outs would probably increase again, if ignoring actually accounted for the decrease. If the teacher reapplies the ignoring strategy, the child's call-outs would probably decrease again.

Multiple baseline designs may also be used with single-subject experiments where

- the same behavior is measured for several students at the same time An example would be observing off-task or out-of-seat behavior among three students in a classroom.
- several behaviors may be measured for one student. The teacher might be observing call-outs, off-task, and out-of seat for a particular child during an observation period
- several settings are observed to see if the same behaviors are occurring across settings. A student's aggressive behavior toward his classmates may be observed at recess, in class, going to or from class, or in the cafeteria.

Norm-Referenced Test--A standardized test in which an individual's performance is compared to the group that was used to calculate the performance standards. Examples would be the CTBS, WISC-R, and Stanford-Binet.

Operational Definition--The description of a behavior and its measurable components. In behavioral observations, the description must be specific and measurable so that the observer will know exactly what constitutes instances and non-instances of the target behavior. Otherwise, reliability may be

Pinpoint--Specifying and describing the target behavior for change in measurable and precise terms. "On time for class" may mean be interpreted as arriving physically in the classroom when the tardy bell has finished ringing or it may mean being at the pencil sharpener, or it may mean being in one's seat and ready to begin work when the bell has finished ringing. Pinpointing the behavior makes it possible to accurately measure the behavior.

Profile--Plotting an individual's behavioral data on a graph

Rate--The frequency of a behavior over a specified time period, such as 5 talk-outs during a 30-minute period, or typing 85 words per minute.

Raw Score--the number of correct responses on a test before they have been converted to standard scores. Raw scores are not meaningful because they have no basis of comparison to the performance of other individuals.

Reliability--The consistency (stability) of a test over time to measure what it is supposed to measure. Reliability is commonly ,measured in four ways:

- Test-retest method-- the test is administered to the same group or individual after a short period of time and the results are compared.
- Alternate form (equivalent form)--measures reliability by using alternative forms to measure the same skills. If both forms are administered to the same group within a relatively short period of time, there should be a high correlation between the two sets of scores if the test has a high degree of reliability.
- Interrater--This refers to the degree of agreement between two or more individuals observing the same behaviors or scoring the same tests.
- Internal reliability is determined by statistical procedures or by correlating one-half of the test with the other half of the test.

Standard Deviation--The standard deviation is a statistical measure of the variability of the scores. The more closely the scores are clustered around the mean, the smaller the SD will be. Test manuals will publish the calculation for the standard deviation.

Standard Error of Measurement--This statistic measures the amount of possible error in a score. If the SEM for a test is + or -3 and the individual's score is 35, than the actual score may be 32 to 38.

Standard Score--a derived score with a set mean (usually 100) and a standard deviation. Examples are T-scores (mean of 50 and a standard deviation of 10), z-scores (mean of 0 and standard deviation of 1), and scaled scores. Scaled scores may be given for age groups or grade levels. IQ scores, for instance, use a mean of 100 and a standard deviation of 15.

Task Analysis--Breaking an academic or behavioral task down into its sequence of steps. Task analysis is necessary when preparing criterion-referenced tests and performing error analysis. A task analysis for a student learning to do laundry might include:

1. Sort the clothes by type (whites, permanent press, delicate)
2. Choose a type and select the correct water temperature and setting
3. If doing a partial load, adjust the water level
4. Measure the detergent
5. Turn on the machine
6. Load the clothes
7. Add bleach, fabric softener at the correct time
8. Wait for the machine to completely stop spinning before opening it.
9. Remove the clothes from the machine and place in dryer.
(A task analysis could be done for drying and folding as well.)

Validity--The degree to which a test measures what it claims to measure, such as reading readiness, self-concept, or math achievement. A test may be highly reliable, but it will be useless if it is not valid. There are several types of validity to examine when selecting or constructing an assessment instrument.

- <u>Content</u> --This type of validity examines the question of whether the types of tasks in the test measure the skill or construct the test claims to measure. That is, a test which claims to measure mastery in algebra would probably not be valid if the majority of the items involved basic operations with fractions and decimals.

- <u>Criterion-referenced validity</u> involves comparing the test results with a valid criterion. For example, a doctoral student preparing a test to measure reading and spelling skills may check the test against an established test such as the WRAT-R or another valid criterion such as school grades.

- Predictive validity refers to how well a test will relate to a future criterion level, such as the ability of a reading test administered to a first-grader to predict that student's performance at third or fifth grade.

- Concurrent validity refers to how well the test relates to a criterion measure given at the same time. For example, a new test which reportedly measures reading achievement may be given to a group which also takes the WRAT-R, which has established validity/ The test results are compared using statistical measures. The recommended coefficient is .80 or better.

- Construct validity refers to the ability of the test to measure a theoretical construct, such as intelligence, self-concept, and other nonobservable behaviors. Factor analysis and correlation studies with other instruments that measure the same construct are ways to determine construct validity.

Skill 3.3 Differentiate between formal/standardized tests and criterion-referenced tests.

Norm-referenced tests compare an individual's score to a specific group. They measure how much a person knows about a certain area rather then what he knows or can do. Norms are based on:

- age-scales, in which the person's performance is compared to the typical performance of a representative group of individuals of the same age. Scales are determined by the number of individuals of various age levels who respond correctly to the test item, or

- point scales, which are calculated for questions of varying levels of difficulty not specifically related to age. Correct responses are totaled to yield a raw score, which, in turn, is converted to a derived score such as age equivalent, grade equivalent, percentile, or standard score.

When interpreting an individual's score on a norm-referenced test, it is important to know the characteristics of the group that was used for the test sample. Tests results for a very specific group of individuals may not be applicable to other groups. Test manuals will give detailed information on sample selection and composition.

Criterion-referenced tests measure a person's mastery of content rather than performance compared to others. Test items are usually prepared from specific educational objectives and may be teacher-made as well as commercially prepared. Scores are measured by the percentage of correct items for a skill (i.e., adding and subtracting fractions of like denominators).

Skill 3.4 Differentiate between the uses of formal/informal assessments.

Formal assessments include norm-referenced tests, commercially prepared inventories, and criterion-referenced tests. These instruments are used primarily for documenting the existence of problems and determining the label for the student (i.e., learning disabled). *Informal assessments* include teacher-made tests, observation, and error analyses. These are mainly used to plan instruction and evaluate student progress on a continual basis. An advantage of using informal assessments is the ease of design and administration, and the usefulness of information the teacher can gain about the student's strengths and weaknesses.

Skill 3.5 Interpret the results of formal/informal academic assessments.

Results of formal assessments are given in derived scores, which compares the student's raw scores to a performance of a specified group of subjects. Criteria for the selection of the group may be based on characteristics such as age, sex, or geographic area. The test results of formal assessments must always be interpreted in light of what type of task the individual was required to perform. The most commonly used derived scores follow.

A. Age and Grade Equivalents. These scores are considered developmental scores because they attempt to convert the student's raw score into an average performance of a particular age or grade group. Age equivalents are expressed in years and months, i.e., 7-3. In the standardization procedure, a mean is calculated for all individuals of the particular age who took the test. If the mean or median number of correct responses for children 7 years and 3 months was 80, then an individual whose raw score was 80 would be assigned an age equivalent of 7 years and 3 months.

Grade Equivalents are written as years and tenths of years, e.g., 6.2 would read sixth grade, second month. Grade equivalents are calculated on the average performance of the group, and have been criticized for their use to measure gains in academic achievement and to identify exceptional students.

Quartiles, Deciles, and Percentiles indicate the percentage of scores that fall below the individual's raw score. Quartiles divide the score distribution into four equal parts; the first quartile is the point at which 25% of the scores fall below, for example. Deciles divide the distribution into ten equal parts; Decile 7 would mark the point below which 70% of the scores fall. Percentiles are the most frequently used, however. A percentile rank of 45 would indicate that the person's raw score was at the point where 45% of the other scores fell below.

B. Standard Scores are raw scores with the same mean (average) and standard deviation (variability of a set of scores). In standardization of a test, about 68% of the scores will fall above or below 1 standard deviation of the mean of 100. About 96% of the scores will fall within the range of 2 standard deviations above or below the mean. A standard deviation of 20, for example, will mean that 68% of the scores will fall between 80 and 120, with 100 as the mean. The most common are T scores, z scores, stanines, and scaled scores. Standard scores are useful because they allow for direct comparison of raw scores from different individuals. In interpreting scores, it is important to note what type of standard score is being used.

C. Criterion Referenced Tests and Curriculum-Based Assessments are interpreted on the basis of the individual's performance on the objectives being measured. Such assessments may be commercially prepared or teacher-made, and can be designed for a particular curriculum or a scope and sequence. These assessments are made by selecting objectives, task analyzing those objectives, and selecting measures to test the skills necessary to meet those tasks. Results are calculated for each objective such as, Cindy was able to divide 2 digit numbers by 1 digit numbers 85% of the time, and was able to divide 2 digit numbers by 2 digit numbers 45% of the time. These tests are useful for gaining insight into the types of error patterns the student makes. Because the student's performance is not compared to others in a group, results are useful for writing IEPs as well as deciding what to teach.

Skill 3.6 Interpret and utilize the results of intelligence tests.

Intelligence tests are relatively good predictors of school performance. Examples are the WISC-R, Detroit Tests of Learning Aptitude-2, and Kaufman Assessment Battery for Children. Some intelligence tests are designed for use with groups, and are used for screening and identification purposes. The individual tests are used for classification and program placement. Since intelligence is a quality that is difficult to precisely define, results of intelligence tests should not be used to discriminate or define the person's potential.

Intelligence test scores should be interpreted in terms of performance, and not the person's potential. The teacher must read the test manuals and become familiar with these items:
- *Areas measured:* verbal, quantitative, memory, cognitive skills?
- *Population:* target age groups, lack of cultural bias, adaptations or norms for children with physical handicaps such as blindness
- *Standardization information*–mean and standard deviation, scaled scores

- *Means of comparing performance between subtests,* such as the Verbal and Performance IQ scores of the WISC-R.
- *Uses of the Results*: The test manual will contain information about the relevant research, suggests uses for the results, and inappropriate uses of the results, i.e., using the K-ABC to identify gifted children.
- *Information on use with special populations,* such as Spanish-speaking, visually impaired, or physically impaired.
- *Information concerning reliability and validity*

Skill 3.7 Interpret \the results of formal/informal social/emotional assessments.

Standardized measures of behavior involve direct observation with a behavior-rating scale. Measurements of emotional states involve inference and subjectivity on the part of the examiner.

A. Behavior Rating Scales

Examples of these scales are the Revised Behavior Problem Checklist, Behavior Rating Profile, and Burks Behavior Rating Scales. Items may be grouped according to categorical characteristics. For the Revised Behavior Problem Checklist, the four major scales are Conduct Disorder, Socialized Aggression, Attention Problem-Immaturity, and Anxiety-Withdrawn, with minor scales of Psychotic Behavior and Motor Excess. Behavior rating scales involve the examiner to rate examples of behaviors on Likert-type scales, such as 0= Not a problem, 1 = mild problem, and 2 = Severe Problem.

Each scale has its own set of scoring procedures; therefore, the teacher must be sure to consult the test manual before attempting to interpret the results. Other factors to consider in interpreting behavior rating scales:

- *Reliability and Validity Information,* norming group information, as well as relevant research on the instrument
- *Sources of information.* Some tests include parent and youth reports or measure behavior across a number of settings in and out of school
- *Suggested uses of the results.* Some tests are intended for screening, but not diagnostic purposes.
- *Scoring and profile information.* For example, the Child Behavior Checklist and Revised Child Behavior Profile lists three social competency scales and behavior problem scales identified by factor analysis for boys and girls in three separate age ranges.

B. Measures of Emotional State These tests are designed to be administered by trained psychologists and psychiatrists. The child's emotional state is inferred by analyzing observable behavior. Types of tests include projective methods, measures of self-concept, and inventories and questionnaires.

Projective Methods. The theory of these methods is that a person will project his or her own meaning, patterns, feelings, and significance to ambiguous stimuli. Because these tests are subjective, it is difficult to establish reliability and validity; therefore, their usefulness for educational purposes is limited. Some examples of these tests are:

- Rorschach Ink Blot Test. The individual states what he "sees" in each of the 10 ink blots. Diagnostic interpretation is based on clinical data.

- Thematic Apperception Test. The examiner uses a series of 31 pictures and asks the child to tell a story about them. The examiner looks for themes in the stories, especially those relating to the main character.

Interpretations of these tests should be read with the following advisories--the reliability and validity, the training of the examiner, and subjective quality.

Self-Concept Measures

Some familiar examples are the Tennessee Self-Concept Scale and Piers-Harris Children's Self-Concept Scale. Most instruments use a system of self-evaluation and self-report. Thus, there is the potential for the child to choose the answer that he or she believes the examiner wants to see. Also, because self-concept is a difficult construct to define, there is the problem of adequate validity.

Inventories and Questionnaires. Many of these are designed for measuring emotional and personality characteristics or adolescents and adults. These tests are often self-report, although some, like the PIC, include a parent report. Results are grouped into scales such as adjustment, achievement, depression, delinquency, and anxiety. These results are generally used with classification and placement decisions. Interpretation of these tests should be done with the issues of reliability and validity. A popular example of this type of test for use with children is the PIC

Personality Inventory for Children (PIC) was designed specifically for evaluating children. The parent completes the inventory of true/false items, and three validity scales are included to determine the "truthfulness" of the responses. 13 of the 30 scales are considered the "profile scales", with the first three--adjustment, achievement, and intellectual screening, considered the "cognitive triad".

Skill 3.8 Interpret the results of formal/informal process assessments.

Formal process assessments tend to center around language reception and expression, which is crucial to school success. Language assessments may measure any or all of these five components:

* *Phonology* involves-aural discrimination of speech sounds and the articulation of those sounds into words.
* *Morphology* is the process of combining phonemes into meaningful words
* *Syntax* refers to the rules for arranging words into sentences.
* *Semantic* tests measure receptive and expressive vocabulary skills.
* *Pragmatics* involves the way that language is used to communicate and interact with others.

An early example of a formal process assessment instrument in the field of learning disabilities is the Illinois Test of Psycholinguistic Abilities, which was modeled after Osgood's communications model. In the ITPA, information is received through auditory or visual "channels". Inside the channels, the information undergoes various processes--*reception*, or input, *association*, organizing and manipulation of the information, and *expression*, the verbal or manual response output. The levels of organization may be automatic (habit or rote processing of information) or representational (symbolic manipulation of information.

The ITPA was organized into six subtests--Visual Reception and Auditory Reception involved the receptive process, the Visual Motor and Auditory-Vocal Association addressed the organizing process, and the expressive process subtests were Motor Expression and Verbal Expression. However, the ITPA was criticized for inadequate reliability and standardization. Today the Test of Language Development measures receptive (listening) and expressive (speaking) skills for in semantics, syntax, and phonology.

Informal process measures are done to gain information about a student's metacognitive knowledge associated with a particular task, such as analyzing visual aids. The teacher gives the student a task involving analysis of visual aids, then interviews the students with direct and open-ended questions. In these interviews, the teacher attempts to answer three questions:

(a) What does the student know about the metagocnitive processes involved in using visual aids? This addresses the student's knowledge of the function of visual aids, and whether the student utilizes background knowledge to predict or clarity the information in the visual aid.

(b) If the student knows that certain strategies are needed to analyze an aid, then does the student know how to perform those strategies?

(c) What variables influence the student's ability or lack of ability to make efficient use of process strategies? (i.e., style of graphic, motivation)

A teacher-made process assessment can be done with a visual aid and a structured, teacher-prepared interview. Interviews begin with global-general questions that measure what the student knows without being prompted to recall specific techniques. Examples of global-general questions are:
* What types of information can graphics tell you?
* What sort of things makes graphics useful?
* What should you do if you can't figure out a graphic?

Following the global-general questions, the teacher can move on to specific questions about specific strategies and components of the strategies. Examples of specific questions would be:
* What does "Identify what is important mean?"
* What does "activating knowledge" mean?

Beginning first with general questions lessens the possibility that the student will answer what he believes the teacher wants to hear. During the specific question stage, the teacher can explore specific aspects of the student's use of the process in more detail.

Skill 3.9 Select and apply appropriate data-based instructional measures.

Data-based instruction is a model of instruction that combines elements of precision teaching, direct-instruction, applied behavior analysis, and criterion-referenced instruction. It features direct and continuous measurement of student progress toward specific instructional objectives. (A detailed discussion of curriculum-based measurement and data-based instruction appears in Mercer and Mercer).

Curriculum-based measurement assesses student progress through continuous rate samples taken from the student's curriculum. CBM is used to establish performance standards for a district or school, identify students who need special instruction interventions, and monitor student progress toward long-term goals.

In CBM data-based instruction, the teacher selects a material at the level which he or she expects the student to have mastered by the end of the school year. Material should be proportionately represented in alternate test forms. A norm-referenced data base can be prepared by comparing the performance of all the students on the same measure. By using several samples, an average score can be computed for the group.

Plotting the data for CBM scores can be done with a box plot to identify extremes. A box plot consists of:

a) ranking the scores from lowest to highest
b) calculating the percentage value of a single score by dividing 1 by the total number of scores in the sample
c) Locate the 90 percent level, the 75% level, , the 25% level, and the 10% level
d) Calculate the median score (50th percentile)
e) Plot the points for individuals above and below the 90 and 10 percentile
f) draw the box for the 75 and 25 percentiles
g) the box plot can be used to determine who should be in a low group, medium group;, and a high group.

With this type of plot, low performers can be identified, students can be divided into groups, instructional programs can be planned, and long-range goals can be established. For low-performing or special education students, this system has applications in establishing a formative evaluation system by using successive higher or lower-level grade materials to calculate current level of functioning from appropriate grade level functioning by comparing the student to normative levels for those grades.

Individual data-based instruction can be done through direct measurement of relevant classroom behaviors such as math computation rate. For permanent products (i.e., class assignments), measurement can be done daily and should be done at least twice weekly. Observational recordings (frequency, rate, duration, time sampling) are useful for classroom behaviors related to successful academic performance. Line graphs and bar graphs are commonly used to plot results. For rate data, ratio graphs plotted on a grid (e.g., correct/incorrect words read during a 1-minute time sample) are often used in applied behavior analysis and precision teaching programs.

For monitoring progress toward long-term instructional goals, performance monitoring charts are prepared for each student. Baseline is the first 3 data collection points. The rate of progress the student is expected to achieve by the end of the first intervention period is represented by a broken line called the trend line. If the student's actual performance is plotted and compared to the trend line. If the student is not making sufficient progress, the teacher will know that a different intervention is needed. A new trend line is established, and the student's progress compared again to the trend. If the student meets the trend, the teacher may continue the instruction method. If the student exceeds the trend, then he or she is considered to have met the criterion, and a new goal proficiency criterion is established.

Short-range goal performance monitoring can be plotted on a mastery monitoring chart. Mastery monitoring is used with precision teaching programs, and charts student progress on a succession of short-term goals. The steps in mastery monitoring are:

⇒ Select the target behavior by administering probe sheets which sample a behavior (e.g., multiplication facts to 5s). Several samples should be collected before the target behavior is established.
⇒ Develop task sheets or probes for daily timed samples of student progress
⇒ Graph data two to five times weekly and decide on a standard of fluency for an instructional goal
⇒ Design the method of instruction
⇒ Analyze the data and make instructional decisions

A proportional chart can show:
⇒ Plots of incorrect responses
⇒ Plots of correct responses
⇒ Progress across several skills, with a vertical line to indicate the change to a new skill,
⇒ A numerical listing of the correct/incorrect responses next to the graph
⇒ Space for writing the behaviors charted, as well as the instructional goal

Data-based instruction and charting can show:
• Changes in level of performance when a new teaching intervention is used
• The rate of change in a trend line
• Consistency or variability in performance
• the measurement of the weekly rate compared to performance aim rate.

Teachers can achieve the most effective use of data-based instruction by following these guidelines in the daily classroom routine::
• Use 1-minute timings for ease of administration and charting
• Initially measure priority behaviors
• Data collection can be done for the whole group
• Set moderately to highly ambitious goals to encourage student achievement

COMPETENCY 4.0 KNOWLEDGE OF READING CURRICULUM AND INSTRUCTION

Skill 4.1 Knowledge of reading curriculum and instruction.

Beginning Reading Approaches

Methods of teaching beginning reading skills may be divided into two major approaches--code-emphasis and meaning emphasis. Both approaches have their supporters and their critics. Advocates of code-emphasis instruction point out that reading fluency depends of accurate and automatic decoding skills, while advocates of meaning emphasis favor this approach for teaching comprehension. Teachers may decide to blend aspects of both approaches to meet the individual needs of their students.

Bottom-up or Code Emphasis Approach:

- Letter-sound regularity is stressed.

- Reading instruction begins with words that consist of letter or letter combinations that have the same sound in different words. Component letter-sound relationships are taught and mastered before introducing new words.

- Examples--phonics, linguistic, modified alphabet, and programmed reading series such as the Merrill Linguistic Reading Program and DISTAR Reading

Top-Down or Meaning-Emphasis Model

- Reading for meaning is emphasized from the first stages of instruction
- Programs begin with words that appear frequently, which are assumed to be familiar and easier to learn. Words are identified by examining meaning and position in context and are decoded by techniques such as context, pictures, initial letters, and word configurations. Thus, a letter may not necessarily have the same sound in different words throughout the story.

- Examples: Whole language, language experience, and individualized reading programs.

Other approaches that follow beginning reading instruction are available to help teachers design reading programs. Choice of approach will depend on the student's strengths and weaknesses. No matter what approach or combination of approaches is used, the teacher should encourage independent reading and build activities into the reading program that stimulate students to practice their skills through independent reading.

Developmental Reading Approaches

Developmental reading programs emphasize daily, sequential instruction. Instructional materials usually feature a series of books, often basal readers, as the core of the program.

1. Basal Reading

Basal reader series form the core of many widely-used reading programs from preprimers through eighth grade... Depending on the series, basals may be meaning-emphasis or code-emphasis. Teacher manuals provide a highly structured and comprehensive scope and sequence, lesson plans, and objectives. Vocabulary is controlled from level to level and reading skills cover word recognition, word attack, and comprehension.

Advantages of basal readers are the structured, sequential manner in which reading is taught. The teacher manuals have teaching strategies, controlled vocabulary, assessment materials, and objectives. Reading instruction is in a systematic, sequential, comprehension-oriented manner.

Many basal reading programs recommend the directed reading activity procedure: for lesson presentation. Students proceed through the steps of motivation, preparation for the new concepts and vocabulary, guided reading and answering questions that give a purpose or goal for the reading; development of strengths through drills or workbook, application of the skills, and evaluation.

A variation of the directed reading method is directed reading-thinking, where the student must generate the purposes for reading the selection, form questions, and read the selection. After reading, the teacher asks questions designed to get the group to think of answers and justify the answers.

Disadvantages of basal readers are the emphasis on teaching to a group rather than the individual. Critics of basal readers claim that the structure may limit creativity and not provide enough instruction on organizational skills and reading for secondary content levels. Basals, however, offer the advantage of a prepared comprehensive program, and may be supplemented with other materials to meet individual needs.

2. Phonics Approach

Word recognition is taught through grapheme-phoneme associations, with the goal of teaching the student to independently apply these skills to new words. Phonics instruction may be synthetic or analytic. In synthetic method, letter sounds are learned first before the student goes on to blending the sounds to form words. The analytic method teaches letter sounds as integral parts of words.

The sounds are usually taught in the sequence: vowels, consonants, consonant blends at the beginning of words (e/g/. b; and dr), and consonant blends at the ends of words (e.g., ld and mp), consonant and vowel digraphs (e.g., ch and sh), and diphthongs (au, oy).

Critics of the phonics approach point out that the emphasis on pronunciation may lead to the student focusing more on decoding than comprehension. Some students may have trouble blending sounds to form words, and others may become confused with words that do not conform to the phonetic "rules". However, advocates of phonics say that the programs are useful with remedial reading and developmental reading. Examples of phonics series are Science Research Associates' *Merrill Phonics* and DLM's *Cove School Reading Program.*

3. Linguistics Approach

In many programs, the whole-word approach is used, meaning that words are taught in word families and as a whole (e.g., cat, hat, rat, pat). The focus is on words instead of isolated sounds Words are chosen on the basis of similar spelling patterns, and irregular spelling words are taught as sight words. Examples of programs using this approach are *SRA Basic Reading Series* and *Miami Linguistic Readers* by D. C. Heath.

Some advantages of this approach are that the student learns that reading is talk written down, and develops a sense of sentence structure. The consistent visual patterns of the lessons guide students from familiar words to semiregular to irregular words. Reading is taught by association with the student's natural knowledge of his own language. Disadvantages are the extremely controlled vocabulary and word by word reading is encouraged. Others criticize the programs for the emphasis on auditory memory skills and the use of nonsense words in the practice exercises.

4. Whole Language Approach

In the whole language approach, reading is taught as a holistic, meaning-oriented activity and is not broken down into a collection of skills. This approach relies heavily on literature or printed matter selected for a particular purpose. Reading is taught as part of a total language arts program, and the curriculum seeks to develop instruction in real problems and ideas. Two examples of whole language programs are *Learning through Literature* (Dodds & Goodfellow) and *Victory!* (Brigance)

Phonics is not taught in a structured, systematic way. Students are assumed to develop their phonetic awareness through exposure to print. Writing is taught as a complement to reading. Writing centers are often part of this program as student learn to write their own stories and read them back, or follow along a cassette of a book while reading along with it.

While the integration of reading with writing is an advantage of the whole language approach, the approach has been criticized for the lack of direct instruction in specific skill strategies. With students with learning problems, more direct instruction may be needed to help students learn the word recognition skills necessary to achieve comprehension.

5. Language Experience Approach

Language experience approach is similar to whole language in that reading is considered as a personal act, literature is emphasized, and students are encouraged to write about their own life experiences. The major difference is that written language is considered a secondary system to oral language, while whole language sees the two as structurally related. Language experience approach is used primarily with beginning readers, but can also be used with older elementary and with older students for corrective instruction. Reading skills are developed along with listening, speaking, and writing skills. The materials are made up of the student's experiences. The philosophy of language experience states:

* What students think about, they can talk about
* What students say, they can write or have someone write
* What students have written or have written for them, they can read.

Development of a language experience story follows this sequence:

Students dictate a story to the teacher in a group activity. Ideas for stories can originate from student artwork, news events, personal experiences, or creative ideas. Topic lists, word cards, or idea lists can also be used to generate topics and ideas for a class story.

The teacher writes down the story in a first draft and the students read them back. The language patterns are the patterns of the students, and they learn to read their own written thoughts. The teacher provide guidance on word choice, sentence structure, and the sounds of the letters and words.

The students edit and revise their story on an experience chart. The teacher provides specific instruction in grammar, sentence structure, and spelling when the need appears, rather than using a specified schedule.

As the students progress, they create their individual story books, adding illustrations if they choose. The story books are place in folders to share with others. Progress is evaluated in terms of the changes in the oral and written expression, as well as mechanics. There is no set method of evaluation student progress, which is one disadvantage of language experience. However, the emphasis on student experiences and creativity stimulates interest and motivation, which is an advantage of the approach.

6. Individualized Reading Approach

The student selects his own reading materials from a variety of materials according to interest and ability, Progress at his or rate. Word recognition and comprehension are taught as the student needs them. The teacher's role is to diagnose errors and prescribe materials, although final choice is up to the student. The individual work can be supplemented by group activities with basal readers and workbooks for specific reading skills. The lack of systematic check of developmental skills and emphasis on self-learning may be a disadvantage for students with learning problems.

Skill 4.2 Recognize the hierarchy of the developmental stages of reading in instruction.

During the preschool years, children acquire cognitive skills in oral language that they apply later on to reading comprehension. Reading aloud to young children is one of the most important things that an adult can do because they are teaching children how to monitor, question, predict, and confirm what they hear in the stories. Reid (1988, p. 165) described four metalinguistic abilities that young children acquire through early involvement in reading activities:

1. *Word consciousness.* Children who have access to books first can tell the story through the pictures. Gradually they begin to realize the connection between the spoken words and the printed words. The beginning of letter and word discrimination begins in the early years.

2. *Language and Conventions of Print.* During this stage children learn the way to hold a book, where to begin to read, the left to right motion, and how to continue from one line to another.

3. *Functions of Print.* Children discover that print can be used for a variety of purposes and functions, including entertainment and information.

4. *Fluency.* Through listening to adult models, children learn to read in phrases and use intonation.

Mercer and Mercer (p. 412) divide the reading experience into two basic processes: word recognition and word and idea comprehension. Reading programs may differ in how and when these skills are presented.

WORD RECOGNITION	WORD AND IDEA COMPREHENSION
Configuration	Vocabulary Development
Content Analysis	Literal Comprehension
Sight Words	Inferential Comprehension
Phonics Analysis	Evaluation or Critical Reading
Syllabication	Appreciation
Structural Analysis	
Dictionary Analysis	

Constructing Meaning from Text

The purpose of reading is to convert visual images (the letters and words) into a message. Pronouncing the words is not enough; the reader must be able to extract the meaning of the text. When people read, they utilize four sources of background information to comprehend the meaning behind the literal text (Reid, p. 166-171).

1. *Word Knowledge:* Information about words and letters. One's knowledge about word meanings is *lexical knowledge*--a sort of dictionary. Knowledge about spelling patterns and pronunciations is *orthographic knowledge.* Poor

readers do not develop the level of automaticity in using orthographic knowledge to identify words and decode unfamiliar words.

2. *Syntax and Contextual Information.* When children encounter unknown words in a sentence, they rely on their background knowledge to choose a word that makes sense. Errors of younger children therefore are often substitutions of words in the same syntactic class. Poor readers often fail to make use of context clues to help them identify words or activate the background knowledge that would help them with comprehension. Poor readers also process sentences word by word, instead of "chunking" phrases and clauses, resulting in a slow pace that focuses on the decoding rather than comprehension. They also have problems answering wh-(Who, what, where, when, why) questions as a result of these problems with syntax.

3. *Semantic Knowledge:* This includes the reader's background knowledge about a topic, which is combined with the text information as the reader tries to comprehend the material. New information is compared to the background information and incorporated into the reader's schema. Poor readers have problems with using their background knowledge, especially with passages that require inference or cause-and-effect.

4. *Text Organization:* Good readers are able to differentiate types of text structure, e.g., story narrative, exposition, compare-contrast, or time sequence. They use knowledge of text to build expectations and construct a framework of ideas on which to build meaning. Poor readers may not be able to differentiate types of text and miss important ideas. They may also miss important ideas and details by concentrating to lesser or irrelevant details.

Characteristics of Good Readers

Research on reading development has yielded information of the behaviors and habits of good readers vs. poor readers. Some of the characteristics of good readers are:

- They think about the information that they will read in the text, formulate questions that they predict will be answered in the text, and confirm those predictions from the information in the text.

- When faced with unfamiliar words, they attempt to pronounce them using analogies to familiar words.

Before reading, good readers establish a purpose for reading, select possible text structure, choose a reading strategy, and make predictions about what will be in the reading.

38

- As they read, good readers continually test and confirm their predictions, go back when something does not make sense, and make new predictions.

COMPETENCY 5.0 KNOWLEDGE OF MATHEMATICS CURRICULUM AND INSTRUCTION

Skill 5.1 Identify basic levels of learning mathematics concepts.

Reid (1988) describes four processes are directly related to an understanding of numbers: Children typically begin learning these processes in early childhood through the opportunities provided by their caretakers. Children who do not get these opportunities have difficulties when they enter school.

- Describing--characterizing an object, set, or event in terms of its attributes, such as calling all cats "kitties", whether they are tigers or house cats

- Classifying--sorting objects, sets, or events, in terms of one or more criteria, such as color, size, or shape--black cats vs. white cats vs. tabbies

- Comparing--determining whether two objects, sets, or events, are alike or different on the basis of a specified attribute, such as differentiating quadrilaterals from triangles on the basis of number of sides.

- Ordering--comparing two or more objects, sets, or events, such as ordering children in a family on the basis of age.

Children usually begin learning about these concepts during early childhood:

- Equalizing--making two or more objects or sets alike on an attribute, such as putting more milk in a glass so it matches the amount of milk in another glass.

- Joining--putting together two or more sets with a common attribute to make one set, such as buying packets of X-Men trading cards to create a complete series.

- Separating--dividing an object or set into two or more sets, such as passing out cookies from a bag to a group of children so that each child gets three cookies.

- Measuring--attaching a number to an attribute, such as three cups of flour, ten gallons of gas.

- Patterns--recognizing, developing, and repeating patterns, such as secret code messages, designs in a carpet or tile floor.

However, most children are not developmentally ready to understand these concepts before they enter school:

- Understanding and working with numbers larger than ten. They may be able to recite larger numbers, but are not able to compare or add them, for example.

- Part-whole concept, or the relationship of a number as part of a larger number

- Numerical notation--place value, additive system, and zero symbol

Children with learning problems often have problems with these concepts after they enter public school because they have either had not had many experiences with developing these basic concepts or they are not developmentally ready to understand such concepts as part-whole, for example.

Sequence of Mathematics Understanding

Children's understanding of mathematics concepts proceeds in a developmental sequence from concrete to semiabstract to abstract. Children with learning difficulties may still be at a concrete or semiabstract level while their peers are ready to work at the abstract level. This developmental sequence has implication for instruction because the teacher will need to incorporate concrete and/or semiabstract levels into lessons for students who did not master these stages of development in their mathematics background. These levels may be explained as follows:

- Concrete: An example of this would be demonstrating 3 + 4 = 7 by counting out three buttons and four buttons to equal seven buttons.

- Semi-Concrete: An example would be using pictures of 3 buttons and 4 buttons to illustrate 3 + 4 = 7.

- Abstract: The student solves 3 + 4 = 7 without using manipulatives or pictures.

In summary, the levels of mathematics content involve:
- Concepts: such as the understanding of number and terms
- Development of mathematics relationships
- Development of mathematics skills such as computation and measuring
- Development of problem-solving ability not only in books, but also environment

Skill 5.2 Recognize and apply knowledge of the sequential development of mathematics skills and concepts.

Mathematics instruction proceeds through a sequential development of skills and concept. For each concept, instruction should proceed from concrete to semiabstract levels before moving on to the abstract level of understanding. This section discusses the skills development of mathematics instruction.

Place Value

This is the basis of our number system. Students need to know that the position of a given number determines its value in our number system. Students need to know the grouping process, the relationship between place and value of a number, that each number to the left is a multiple of 10, and that there is only one digit per position in our number system.

Addition and Subtraction

These are the first mathematics that students are expected to learn. This requires not only an understanding of place value, but knowledge of the basic addition facts. Addition is conceptualized as the union of two sets.

Subtraction is more difficult because it has three different interpretations:

a. *Taking away* a quantity from another. (Zoe has 10 stickers. She gives 5 away to her friend Jamie. How many stickers does Zoe have left?)

b. *Comparison*—how much more one quantity is than another. (Tom and Matt are selling chocolate bars for the school band. In the first week, Tom sold 136 chocolate bars and Matt sold 97. How many more chocolate bars has Tom sold than Matt?)

c. *Missing addend* —how much more of a quantity is needed. (Jeff is saving his money to buy a video game. The game costs $35.99 on sale. Jeff has 29.50 so far. How much more does he need to buy the video game?)

Multiplication and Division

There are different ways of interpreting these operations. Different students will find certain interpretations easier to understand then others. An understanding of the different ways of conceptualizing these operations will help the teacher adjust instruction for individual needs. Students need a mastery of addition and subtraction facts in order to do well in multiplication and division, which are extensions of these operations. The division algorithm is the most difficult for students to learn.

Multiplication may be viewed in five different ways:

1) *Repeated addition*-- 7 x 5 could be viewed as 7 + 7 +7 + 7 + 7 = 35

2) *Arrays*--7 X 5 is depicted as 7 rows of 5 objects or 5 rows of 7 objects, like rows of seats in a classroom

3) *Cartesian product of two sets*--This interpretation is used with problems such as, "Maria goes to Baskin Robbins for an ice cream cone. She decided to buy a two-scoop cone and has 25 flavors to choose from. How many possible combinations can Maria make?" There are 50 possible combinations because 25 choices x 2 scoops of ice cream = 50 combinations.

4) *Linear Prototypes*--The problem 7 x 5 can be shown on a number line by starting with 0 and skipping 5 spaces 7 times, stopping on 35.

5) *Multiple Sets*--12 x 6 can be described in a problem like this: Jamal is buying pencils for school for himself and his two brothers. He buys 6 packages of pencils. Each package has 12 pencils. How many pencils did Jamal buy? (12 x 6 = 72.)

Division can be conceptualized in two ways: For a problem 32 divided by 8 = 4--

1) Measurement--the problem may be seen as 8 groups of 4. A sample problem could read, "Michelle has a 32-inch piece of yarn. She needs 8-inch pieces for her string art project. How many pieces can she cut from the yarn?" (The yarn is measured into equal parts.)

2) Partition--the problem may be seen as 8 dots in each of 4 groups. A sample problem could read, "32 students to on a field trip to a museum. They are assigned to 4 tour guides for the guided tour. If the tour guides have an equal number of students in their groups, how many students are in each group?" (The total group of 32 is broken up into 4 equal groups.)

Fractions

Fractions may be interpreted as:

* *a part of the whole* (probably the most familiar)--"Stacey is sharing a mushroom pizza with 3 friends. If everyone gets an equal share, what part of the pizza will each girl get?" Answer: 1/4.

* *a subset of a parent set*--"Josh's dog had 8 puppies. 3 puppies are white with spots. What fraction of the puppies are white with spots?" Answer: 3/8.

* *a ratio*--Examples of ratios could be 2 girl for every 3 boys in a class.

Decimal Fractions and Percents

Decimal fractions and percents are an the extension of place value system and common fractions. Students who have not mastered operations with common fractions will probably also have trouble with understanding decimal fractions and percents, as well as converting one to another.

Problem Solving

The skills of analysis and interpretation are necessary to problem solving. Students with learning problems often find problem solving difficult, with the result that they avoid problem-solving activities. Skills necessary for successful problem solving include:

1) Identification of the main idea--what is the problem about?

2) Main question of the problem--what is the problem asking for?

3) Identifying important facts--what information is necessary to solve?

4) Choose a strategy and an operation--How will the student solve the problem and with what operation?

5) Solve the problem--Perform the computation

6) Check for accuracy of computation and compare the answer to the main question. Does it sound reasonable?

7) If solution is incorrect, repeat the steps.

Secondary Mathematics

Other topics of mathematics that are important to develop, especially as the student enters the higher grades, are spatial relationships, measurements, and patterns. Instruction in these areas allows students to discover relationships and properties of three-dimensional objects, explore the logical nature of mathematics, and build a foundation for algebra and geometry. Secondary students also need instruction in consumer mathematics (ration, proportion, interest, percent, and consumer credit) because students will need to balance checkbooks, calculate best buys, apply for credit, compare interest rates, and budget their money. Students will need to know the mathematics involved with loans, credit cards, mortgages, and taxes.

COMPETENCY 6.0 KNOWLEDGE OF SPELLING CURRICULUM AND INSTRUCTION

Skill 6.1 Identify basic instructional approaches to spelling.

Spelling instruction should include words misspelling in daily writing, generalizing spelling knowledge, and mastering objectives in progressive phases of development. Developmental stages of spelling are:

1) *Prephonemic Spelling*--Children know that letters stand for a message, but they do not know the relationship between spelling and pronunciation

2) *Early Phonemic Spelling*--Children are beginning to understand spelling. They usually write the beginning letter correctly, with the rest consonants or long vowels.

3) *Letter-Name Spelling*--Some words are consistently spelled correctly. The student is developing a sight vocabulary and a stable understanding or letters as representing sounds. Long vowels are usually used accurately, but silent vowels are omitted. Unknown words are spelled by the child attempting to match the name of the letter to the sound.

4) *Transitional Spelling*--This phase is typically entered in late elementary school. Short vowel sounds are mastered and some spelling rules known. They are developing a sense of which spellings are correct and which are not.

5) *Derivational Spelling*--This is usually reached from high school to adulthood. This is the stage where spelling rules are being mastered.

INSTRUCTIONAL APPROACHES

Rule-Based Instruction. Spelling is taught as a system of rules and generalizations. Rule-based instruction may be taught with the linguistics or phonics approach.

A. The *linguistic approach* is based on the idea that there is regularity in the phoneme/grapheme correspondence. Spelling rules, generalizations, and patterns are taught that apply to whole words, and the spelling lists are selected according to a particular pattern. (e.g., take, cake, rake, fake)

B. _The phonics approach_ teaches the student to associate a sound with a particular letter or combination of letters. The student breaks the words broken down into syllables, pronounces each syllable, and writes the letters that represent the sound. Rules that apply to a large number of words are taught first. After the students generalize these rules, exceptions are taught.

Multisensory Approaches. Multisensory approaches to spelling are based on the principle that spelling incorporates _visual skills_ (seeing the word and discriminating the letters), _auditory recognition_ of the word, and _motor skills_ (writing). Supporters of multisensory approaches assert that students who learn to spell using these approaches can use any of these modalities to recall the word and are better able to remember the words. Several more popular methods are described here:

1. Fernald Method. This method is also called VAKT, because it uses visual, auditory, kinesthetic, and tactile modalities. According to this method, learning to spell involves a clear perception of the word, development of a clear visual image, and repetition of the word until the motor pattern becomes automatic. Words are taught in this sequence:

* Teacher writes and says the word; students listen and watch
* Student traces the word while saying it, then writes the word while saying I
* Student writes the word from memory. If the word is incorrect, the steps are repeated. If it is correct, the word is put in a file box to use in stories.
* The tracing method may be discontinued at later stages if it is not needed.

2. Gillingham method. The Gillingham method teaches letter/sound correspondence with an alphabetic system. Words are learned syllable by syllable. Spelling words are studied by "simultaneous oral spelling". The teacher says the word and the student repeats the word, names the letters while writing them, and then reads the written word. The method differs from Fernald because the words that are taught are selected according to a structural sequence, and individual letters and sounds are emphasized, rather than whole words.

3. Cover-and-Write. The student follows four steps in learning a word.
* Look at the word and say it.
* Write the word twice while looking at it.
* Cover the word and write it again.
* Check the spelling by looking at it.
Repeat if needed.

Test-Study-Test. At the beginning of a spelling unit, students are given a pretest. Words that the students misspell become individual study lists. At the end of the unit, the students are tested again. Any misspelled words become the basis for the next study list. Periodic checks are conducted to determine if any words need to be reintroduced. It is recommended that students correct their own tests with the teacher's supervision. Mastery checks also include samples of the students' writing to make sure that students can spell the words in their actual writing.

Fixed- and Flow Word Lists. Fixed lists present a new list of words, usually assigned on a weekly basis. The words may or may not be familiar to the students. The problem with fixed lists is that the words the student continues to misspell may be ignored or left for the student to practice as soon as the next list is assigned. In a flow list, words are dropped as the student learns to spell them and new words are added. The teacher periodically re-tests the student for retention and may add words back as needed.

Imitation Methods. The method is used with students who have not had success with traditional methods. The teacher provides an oral and written model of the target word. The student imitates the model by spelling the word and writing. The procedure is repeated until the student can write the word correctly without models and prompts. Mastery checks are conducted at the units.

COMPETENCY 7.0 KNOWLEDGE OF ORAL LANGUAGE CURRICULUM AND INSTRUCTION

Skill 7.1 Recognize the normal sequence of language development.

Language is the means whereby people communicate their thoughts, request information, and respond to others. Communication competence is an interaction of cognitive competence, social knowledge, and language competence. Communication problems may result from problems in any or all of these areas directly impact the student's ability to interact with others. Language consists of several components, each of which follows a sequence of development.

Brown and colleagues (p. 144, in Reid, 1988) were the first to describe language learning as function of developmental stages rather than age. He developed a formula to group the mean length of utterances (sentences) into stages. Counting the number of morphemes per 100 utterances, one can calculate a mean length of utterance, or MLU:

Total number of morphemes/100 = MLU; e.g., 180/100 = 1.8

Summary of Brown's findings about MLU and language development:

Stage	MLU	Developmental Features
I	1.5-2.0	14 basic morphemes (e.g., in, on, articles, possessives)
II	2.0-2.5	Beginning of pronoun use, auxiliary verbs
III	2.5-3.0	Language form approximate adult forms Beginning of questions and negative statements
IV	3.0-3.5	Use of complex (embedded) sentences
V	3.5-4.0	Use of compound sentences

COMPONENTS OF LANGUAGE

Language learning is composed of five components. Children progress through developmental states through each component.

Phonology

Phonology is the system of rules about sounds and sound combinations for a language. A phoneme is the smallest unit of sound that combines with other sounds to make words. By itself a phoneme does not have a meaning; it must be combined with other phonemes. Problems in phonology may be manifested as developmental delays in acquiring consonants or reception problems, such as misinterpreting words because a different consonant was substituted.

Morphology

Morphemes are the smallest units of language that convey meaning. Morphemes are root words, or free morphemes that can stand alone (e.g.,. walk), and affixes (e.g., ed, s, ing). Content words carry the meaning in a sentence, and functional words join phrases and sentences. Generally, students with problems in this area may not use inflectional endings in their words, may not be consistent in their use or certain morphemes, or may be delayed in learning morphemes such as irregular past tenses

Syntax

Syntax rules, commonly known as grammar, govern how morphemes and words are correctly combined, Wood (1976) describes six stages of syntax acquisition: (Mercer, p. 347)

- *Stages 1 and 2*--Birth to about 2: Child is learning the semantic system.

- *Stage 3*--Ages 2 to 3: Simple sentences contain subject and predicate.

- *Stage 4*--About 2 1/2 to 4: Elements such as question words are added to basic sentences (e.g., where), word order is changed to ask questions. The child begins to use "and" to combine simple sentences, and child begins to embed words within the basic sentence.

- *Stage 5*--about 3 1/2 to 7 years. The child uses complete sentences that include word classes of adult language. The child is becoming aware of appropriate semantic functions of words and differences within the same grammatical class.

♦ *Stage 6*--About 5 to 20 years--Child begins to learn complex sentences and sentences that imply commands, requests, and promises.

Syntactic deficits are manifested by the child using sentences that lack length or complexity for a child that age. They may have problems understanding or creating complex sentences and embedded sentences.

Semantics

Semantics is language content: objects, actions, and relations between objects. As with syntax, Wood (1976) outlines stages of semantic development:

- *Stage I*--birth to about 2 years. Child is learning the meaning while learning the first words. Sentences are one-word, but the meaning varies according to the context. Therefore, "doggie" may mean "This is my dog.", "There is a dog", or "The dog is barking".

- *Stage 2*--About 2 years to 8 years. Child progresses to two-word sentences about concrete actions. As more words are learned, the child forms longer sentences, although until about age 7, things are defined in terms of visible actions. Children begin to respond to prompts (e.g., pretty/flower), and about age 8, can respond to a prompt with an opposite (e.g., pretty--ugly)

- *Stage 3*--Begins about age 8. Child's word meanings that relate directly to experiences, operations, and processes. Vocabulary is defined by the child's experiences, not the adult's. About age 12, the child begins to give "dictionary" definitions, and semantic level approaches that of an adults.

Semantic problems take the form of:

- limited vocabulary

- inability to understand figurative language or idioms; interprets literally

- failure to perceive multiple meanings of words, changes in word meaning from changes in context, resulting in incomplete understanding or what is read

- difficulty understanding linguistic concepts (e.g., before/after), verbal analogies, and logical relationships such as possessives, spatial, and temporal

- misuse of transition words such as "although", "regardless"

51

Pragmatics

Commonly known as the speaker's intent, pragmatics is used to influence or control actions or attitudes of others. Communicative competence depends on how well one understands the rules of language, but also the social rules of communication such as taking turns and using the correct tone of voice.

Pragmatic deficits are manifested by failures to respond properly to indirect requests after age 8 (e.g., "Can't you turn down the TV?" elicits a response of "No", instead of "Yes", and the child turning down the volume.). Children with these deficits have trouble reading cues that indicate the listener does not understand them. Whereas a person would usually notice this and adjust one's speech to the listener's needs, the child with pragmatic problems does not do this.

Pragmatic deficits are also characterized by inappropriate social behaviors such as interruptions or monopolizing conversations. Children may use immature speech and have trouble sticking to a topic These problems can presses into adult, affecting academic, vocational, and social interactions.

Problems in language development often require long-term interventions, and can persist into adulthood. Certain problems are associated with different grade levels:

Preschool and Kindergarten: The child's speech may sound immature, the child may not be able to follow simple directions, and often cannot name things such as days of the week and colors. They may not be able to discriminate between sounds and associate letters with sounds. The may substitute sounds and have trouble responding accurately to certain types of questions. They may play less with peers or participate in nonplay or parallel play.

Elementary students: Problems with sound discrimination persists, and the child may have problem with temporal and spatial concepts (e.g., before-after). As the child progresses though school, the child may have problems making the transition from narrative to expository writing. Word retrieval problems may not be very evident because the child begins to devise strategies to such as talking around the word he or she cannot remember, using fillers, and descriptors. They may speak more slowly, have problems sounding out words, and get confused with multiple-meaning words. Pragmatic problems show up in social situations such as failure to correctly interpret social cues and adjust their language accordingly, inability to predict consequences, and formulate requests to obtain new information.

Secondary students' difficulties become more subtle; they lack the ability to use and understand higher-level syntax, semantics, and pragmatics. If they have problems with auditory language, they may have trouble with short-term memory. Receptive and/or expressive language delays impair their ability to learn effectively. They often lack the ability to organize and categorize the information they receive in school. Problems associated with pragmatic deficiencies persist, but because they are often aware of their problems, frustration, withdrawal, or inattention occurs.

Skill 7.2 Recognize the sociocultural influences of speech and language development.

Hispanic children represent the fastest-growing minority and approximately 3/4 of the children designated as limited English proficiency (LEP). Additionally, culturally diverse students may speak a dialect of a language such as Spanish, which has its own system of pronunciations and rules. It should be stressed that speaking a dialect does **not in itself** mean that the child has a language problem. Certain English sounds and grammar structures may not have equivalents in some languages, and failure to produce these elements may be a function of inexperience with English rather than a language delay.

When minority or culturally diverse children are being screened for language problems, learning disabilities, or other exceptional student programs, the tests and assessment procedures must be **nondiscriminatory**. Furthermore, testing should be done in the child's native language; however, if school instruction has not been in the native language, there may appear to be a problem because assessments typically measure school language. Even with native English-speaking children, there are differences between the language that is functional at home and community and the language requirements of school.

COMPETENCY 8.0 KNOWLEDGE OF CURRICULUM AND INSTRUCTION FOR WRITTEN EXPRESSION

Skill 8.1 Recognize the components of written language.

The prime objective of handwriting is legibility. While younger elementary children may exhibit letter reversals, poor spacing, omissions, and poorly formed letters in their writing, they are not considered a writing problem unless they persist over time and the student does not improve in simple writing tasks.

Components of written language that may be assessed include:

A. Fluency--number of words written, including sentence length and complexity. Fluency is related to age; the average number of words per sentences increases with age by 1 word per year from an average of 8 words for an 8 year-old up to about age 13.

B. Syntax --Syntactic errors include word omissions, incorrect word error, incorrect verb and pronoun usage, and lack of punctuation. Syntax is measured by categorizing and counting the number of sentences in four categories: incomplete fragment, simple, compound, and complex. With age, students should decrease fragments and simple sentences. The T-unit is another measure of syntax. T-units are the shortest grammatically correct segment that a passage can be divided into without creating fragments. A simple sentence, for example, would be 1 T-unit, while a compound sentence can be 2. By counting the total number of words written by the number of T-units, a ratio can be calculated. Again, with age, the average T-unit length should increase throughout the school years.

C. Vocabulary. This refers to originality and maturity in choice of words, as well as the variety of words. In a Type-Token Ratio, the ratio is calculated by the total number of different words (types) divided by the total number of words used (tokens). An index of diversification may also be calculated by dividing the total number of words by the number of times the word used most often (e.g., *the)* appears. A third measure of vocabulary can be done by comparing words from a sample of the student's written expression with a list of words commonly used by other students (i.e., the Dolch list). Typically, the diversity of the student's vocabulary should increase with age and experience.

D. Structure. This involves grammar, punctuation, and capitalization. Structural errors can be analyzed by type of error. The Grammatical Correctness Ratio (Stuckless and Marks, 1966 in Mercer, 558). can be calculated by: (a) sleeting 50 words from a composition, (b) counting the number of grammatical errors (c) subtracting this number from 50, (d) dividing the result

54

by 50, and (e) multiplying the quotient by 100 to yield a percent, which allows the ratio to be used as a basis of comparison with previous scores.

E. <u>Content</u>: Consists of accuracy, ideas, and organization. Aspects of content development involve knowing the purpose of the writing, the intended audience, and the subject matter. Personal aspects of the writer, such as intelligence, previous life experiences, language development, and motivation also act as factors in the quality of the written work produced.

Skill 8.2 Identify the sequence of development of written expression skills.

Composition should be taught as a process rather than a product. The first step in learning composition is having access to literature and writing materials. When adults read aloud to children, the children learn about styles of literature and the function of print and pictures in a book. Having access to paper and writing materials give children opportunities to experiment with drawing and writing. When children enter school, they can learn to write notes, label pictures, and keep journals.

Most of the writing children do at school is business-related, or transactional writing. Transactional writing includes expository (explaining subjects or procedures), descriptive (helps the reader visualize the topic), or persuasive (explaining a point of view). Students may also do expressive writing or poetic writing, which requires a knowledge of formal literary style. Initially, students may be resistant to writing, especially expressive writing, because they may be afraid to show their feelings or make mistakes. Journals are especially helpful to encourage students to practice expressive writing.

Writing should be taught as a process, not a product. Free writing will help reduce writing anxiety. Having children participate in journals and free writing will help build confidence. Writing should be integrated into all subject areas, and the atmosphere should be positive. Writing should be fun, and include a variety of types of writing. Children's writing should be shared with others for feedback and for enjoyment.

Each phase of the writing process has strategies that help the student develop metacognitive skills and proficiency. Instruction should not just focus on the mechanics (grammar, punctuation, spelling) of writing, but also on developing fluency and positive feelings about the process.
:

Prewriting--the planning phase. During preplanning, the student must decide on a purpose, find a topic, establish an audience, decide how the paper will be organized, and experiment with ideas. Strategies for generating ideas can be done individually or as a group activity and include:

- Listing
- Brainstorming--gathering ideas about the topic
- Interest Inventories
- Free writing

Organizing content includes graphic approaches that present the relationships of ideas visually:
- Mapping
- Webbing
- Clustering
-

Drafting: In this phase, ideas are developed and the writer makes connections between the ideas. During this phase, mechanics should not be considered, and the student should not spend too much time in this phase. Learner activities include:

- Focus on the ideas, not the content
- Consult the teacher or peer about the content
- Read the piece or a portion to defocus and generate new ideas

Revising: After the drafts have been written, the student may reorganize ideas, select ideas for further development, and edit the paper for mistakes in grammar and spelling. Sections of the paper may be removed or reordered.
Strategies include:

- Putting the paper aside for a day or two
- Asking the teacher or a peer for feedback
- Use scissors and tape to reorganize sections of the paper
- Use the computer to aid in revision

Final draft: The writer gives the paper a final editing, reads the paper to see that everything makes sense, and makes last corrections before turning the paper in. Some of the things that a student can do to prepare the final draft are--

- Use a checklist to check the final copy for errors
- Read the story into a tape recorder and play it back with a written copy to listen for grammatical errors and pauses where punctuation belongs
- Read the paper one sentence at a time to identify sentence fragments

COMPETENCY 9.0 KNOWLEDGE OF CONTENT AREAS

Skill 9.1 Identify basic instructional approaches for content areas.

Instructional alternatives to help students with learning problems may be referred to as compensatory techniques, instructional adaptations, or accommodation techniques. A problem-solving approach to determining what modifications should be made center around: (a) the requirements of the course, (b) the requirements that the student is not meeting, (c) factors interfering with the student's meeting the requirements, (d) and identify possible modifications.

The classroom teacher can modify the instructional environment in several areas:

I. *Classroom Organization*: The teacher can vary grouping arrangements (e.g., large group, small group, peer tutoring., or learning centers) and methods of instruction (teacher-directed or student-directed)

II. *Classroom Management*: The teacher can vary grading systems, vary reinforcement systems, and vary the rules (differentiate for some students).

    A. Methods of Presentation: Variation of methods include--
    B. Content--amount to be learned, time to learn, and concept level
    C. General Structure--advance organizers, immediate feedback, memory devices, and active involvement of students
    D. Type of presentation--verbal or written, transparencies, audio-visual

III. *Methods of Practice*:
    A. General Structure: amount to be practiced, time to finish, group, individual, or teacher-directed, and vary level of difficulty
    B. Level of response: copying, recognition, or recall with and without cues
    C. Types of Materials: worksheets, audio-visual, texts

IV. *Methods of Testing*
    A. Type: Verbal, written, or demonstration
    B. General structure: time to complete, amount to complete, group or individual testing
    C. Level of response: multiple choice, essay, recall of facts

Presentation of Subject Matter

Subject Matter should be presented in a fashion that helps students <u>organize</u>, <u>understand</u>, and <u>remember</u> important information. Advance organizers and other instructional devices can help students to:
- connect information to what is already known.
- make abstract ideas more concrete,
- capture students' interest in the material
- help students to organize the information and visualize relationships

Organizers can be visual aids such as diagrams, tables, charts, guide, or verbal cue that alerts the student to the nature and content of the lesson. Organizers may be used:

⇒ <u>before</u> the lesson to alert the student to the main points of the lesson, establish a rationale for learning, and activate background information
⇒ <u>during</u> the lesson to help students organize the information, keep focused on the important points, and aid comprehension
⇒ <u>at the close</u> of the lesson to summarize and remember important points

Examples of organizers include:
⇒ Question and graphic-oriented study guides
⇒ Concept diagramming: students brainstorm a concept and organize information into 3 lists (always present, sometimes present, and never present)
⇒ Semantic feature analysis: students construct a table with examples of the concept in the vertical column and important features or characteristics in the horizontal column.
⇒ Semantic webbing: the concept is placed in the middle of the chart or chalkboard and relevant information is placed around it. Lines connect and demonstrate the relationships.
⇒ Memory (mnemonic) devices
⇒ Diagrams, charts, and tables

Skill 9.2 Recognize techniques for modifying content areas.

Materials, usually textbooks, are usually modified because of reading level. The goal of modification is to present the material in a manner that the student can more easily understand while preserving the basic ideas and content. Modifications of course material may take the form of:

Simplifying Texts

a) Using a highlighter to mark key terms, main ideas, and concepts. In some cases, a marker may be used to delete nonessential content.
b) *Cut and Paste*. The main ideas and specific content are cut and pasted on separate sheets of paper. Additional headings or other graphic aids can be inserted to help the student understand and organize material
c) Supplement with *graphic aids or tables*
d) Supplement text with *study guides, questions, and directed preview*
e) Use *self-correcting materials*
f) Allow *additional time* or *break content material* into smaller, more manageable units.

Taped Textbooks

Textbooks can be taped by the teacher or aide for student to follow along. In some cases, the student may qualify for recordings of textbooks from agencies such as Recordings for the Blind.

Parallel Curriculum

Projects such as Parallel Alternative Curriculum (PAC) or Parallel Alternative Strategies for Students (PASS)., which present the content at a lower grade reading level and come with tests, study guides, vocabulary activities, and tests.

Supplementary Texts

Book publishers such as Steck-Vaughn publish series of content-area texts that have been modified for reading level, amount of content presented on pages, highlighted key terms, and visual aids.

Modifications for Assessment

Test-taking is not a pleasant experience for many students with behavioral and/or learning problems. They may lack study skills, may experience anxiety before or during a test, or may have problems understanding and differentiating the task requirements for different tests. The skills necessary to be successful vary with the type of test. Certain students have difficulties with writing answers, but may be able to express their knowledge of subject matter verbally. Therefore, modifications of content area material may be extended to methods and modifications for evaluation and assessment of student progress.

Some of the ways that teachers can modify assessment for individual needs include:

59

- Help students get used to timed tests with timed practice tests.
- Provide study guides before tests.
- Makes tests easier to read by leaving ample space between the questions.
- Modify multiple choice tests by reducing the number of choices, reforming questions to yes-no, or using matching items
- Modify short-answer tests with cloze (fill-in) statements or provide a list of facts or choices that the student can choose from.
- Essay tests can be modified by using partial outlines for the student to complete, allowing additional time, or test items that do not require extensive writing

Homework

Homework provides students with an opportunity for independent practice and review of the day's lesson. Homework develops the self-discipline and study skills necessary for success in secondary and post-secondary settings. However, getting students with behavioral and learning problems to complete homework assignments is often a problem for their teachers. As a result, homework may not be regularly assigned and incorporated into the grading process. Teachers who do not give prompt feedback may give their students the impression that homework doesn't really count much. Encouraiging motivation for homework also can be done by planning and alternating assignments that can sometimes be done in class, be done as a group or individually, or done at home.

Mercer and Mercer suggest best practices for assigning and incorporating homework into the learning process:

* Homework should be appropriate for the student's age and academic levels--
    Grades 1 to 3--One to three 15-minute assignments weekly
    Grades 4 to 6--Two to four 15- to 45-minute assignments weekly
    Grades 7 to 9--Up to five 45- to 75-minute assignments weekly
    Grades 10-12--Up to five 75- to 120 minute assignments weekly

* Homework should be an integral part of the learning process, not busy work or used as a punishment.

* Homework assignments must be matched to the students' ability and skill level.

* Explain the instructions clearly and provide some guided practice for the homework before the students take it home.

* Evaluation should be done promptly, and maintain a cumulative record of student's progress on homework.

* Homework completion should be reinforced with praise or contingency rewards.

* Involve parent participation and support for homework.

* Facilitate homework with support systems such as peer tutoring, administrative support, computer, parent support.

COMPETENCY 10. 0   KNOWLEDGE OF SOCIAL/AFFECTIVE SKILLS.

Skill 10.1   Identify age-appropriate social/affective skills for individuals and groups.

One of the components of Bower's definition of emotional handicaps is an inability to form satisfactory interpersonal relationships with others. Social skill deficits may compound academic problems because time spent engaged in negative encounters with others or maladaptive behavior takes valuable time away from learning. Many children with behavior disorders display deficits in such areas as popularity with others, ability to accept authority and rules, ability to get along with others, ability to adapt to changes and demands of different situations. Social skills instruction also included "survival skills" such as asking for assistance, communication skills, and problem-solving.

Possible reasons for social skills deficits may be:

* Lack of suitable role models (e.g., family members who consistently display aggression to resolve conflicts)
* Lack of opportunity to observe and practice certain social skills (e.g., a young child who has not had much interaction with children may find it difficult to take turns in games)
* Lack of previous instruction in certain skills (e.g., a child who has never had to travel on public transportation will probably not know how to read schedules and ask for help in using public transportation.)
* Cultural differences which may create conflicts but may not in themselves be maladaptive (i.e., differences in "personal space" boundaries between persons having a conversation)

Methods of identifying and assessing social skills deficits include:

1. Social Skill Checklists. Examples of commercial checklists include the Walker Problem Behavior Identification Checklist, Revised Behavior Problem Checklist, and the Devereux scales for elementary and adolescent children. Checklists are used to report the presence or absence of a behavior, while rating scales indicate the frequency of a particular behavior and often include teacher as well as parent report forms.

2. Direct observation of the child in various settings to identify problem behaviors across settings. The child's behavior can also be compared to that of his or her peers in similar settings. Observations should include the components of the child's environment as well as how others interact with the child. It is possible that adjustments in the environment can decrease or eliminate the undesirable behavior.

3. Role Playing. In this type of observation, a social situation is staged, and the teacher observes the student's behavior. The teacher can determine if the student does not know the skill, or knows the skill but does not practice it. Role plays may be part of commercially prepared training problems, or designed by the teacher.

4. Self-Reports. The student may complete a checklist, a questionnaire, sentences with open-ended statements, or a direct interview with the teacher.

5. Sociometric measures Three basic formats are (a) peer nominations based on nonbehavioral criteria such as preferred playmates, (b) peer ratings, where students rate all of their peers on nonbehavioral criteria such as work preferences, and (c) peer assessments, where peers are rated with respect to specific behaviors.

Skill 10.2 Apply interventions that promote age-appropriate social skills for individuals and/or groups.

Mercer and Mercer (1993) recommend five general teaching techniques to build positive self-concepts in students and can do much to eliminate the frustration, anxiety, and resulting acting-out behaviors in children. These suggestions are:

- Incorporate learning activities that provide opportunities for success
- Establish goals and expectations
- Monitor progress and provide regular feedback
- Provide positive and supportive learning environment
- Teach students to be independent learners

There are commercial programs to teach specific social skills, but the teacher can take advantage of opportunities throughout the day to teach social skills. Examples of such opportunities include:

- Teacher modeling of positive social behaviors throughout the day
- Reinforcing instances when students display positive behaviors
- Planning instances for students to practice social behaviors
- Assigning students responsibilities
- Assisting students to identify strengths and target behaviors for changes
- Assist students to set goals and make plans to reach those goals

Teaching techniques that have been used to teach social skills include:

1. *Bibliotherapy*—Selected children's books are used to help the child identify with the problems faced with the main character, release emotions regarding the

problems, and develop insight into his own behavior. Through reading about others with similar problems, the child can discuss the situation in the book, relate them to his own situation, and analyze the problem-solving methods used in the story.

2. *Attribution Retraining* --Often, students with learning and behavior problems attribute their success or failure to outside causes rather than their own ability or lack of effort. Through attribution retraining, students are taught to attribute success to their own efforts (i.e., studying rather than the test being too easy) and failure to ineffective strategies, rather than being "dumb". Students are taught study skills and other learning strategies to help them become better learners.

3,. *Modeling*: The teacher reinforces students to exhibit the desirable behaviors as well as models positive social skills in his individual behavior. For example, if the teacher wants students to learn how to initiate a conversation, he can select the student models, set up a demonstration of appropriate ways to initiate a conversation, and have the other students observe the model. The teacher should provide opportunities for the students to practice, and consistently reinforce students who perform the behavior.

4. *Behavior Modification*: Behavior modification is discussed more extensively in the section in Competency 14.

5. *Cognitive Behavior Modification*: Meichenbaum's research in this technique is well-known in the field of learning disabilities. CBM involves a three-step process to teach academic as well as social skills. The goal of CBM is to encourage the student to think through his or her actions before acting. In the CBM process,

a) the teacher or another adult performs the task or social skill while verbalizing the thinking process aloud
b) the student performs the task or social skill while verbalizing the process aloud, while the teacher reinforces and provides feedback
c) the student performs the task while thinking to himself, and the teacher provides reinforcement and feedback

As part of this process, the teacher should build in errors or obstacles in order to teach students how to deal with mistakes and setbacks.

6. *Self-Management*: Self-management is an important part of social skills training, especially for older students preparing for employment. Components of self-management include:
a) self-monitoring--choosing behaviors and alternatives and monitoring those actions

b) self-evaluation--deciding the effectiveness of the behavior in solving the problem
c) self-reinforcement--telling yourself that you are capable of success

7. *Interview techniques* such as Life-space Interviewing and Reality Therapy These techniques assist the student to solve interpersonal problems and manage crisis situations through discussing the problem and the maladaptive behaviors, generating alternatives, and assuming responsibility for one's actions.

8. *Commercial Programs.* Examples of these programs include:
- Asset: A Social Skills Program for Adolescents
- CLASS--Contingencies for Learning Academic and Social Skills
- Getting Along with Others
- Skillstreaming and Elementary School Child and Skillstreaming the Adolescent
- Social Skills for Daily Living
- Coping With Series
- Walker Social Skills Curriculum, which includes ACCEPTS and ACCESS.

These programs teach skills such as friendship skills (i.e., giving compliments), problem-solving (asking for help), successful classroom behaviors (complying with rules), conversation skill (asking questions), and skills for difficult situations (rejection by peers, criticism from an employer). Teaching is usually done through a process of
- providing a description of the behavior and rationale for learning the appropriate behavior
- modeling of the behavior
- rehearsal and practice
- feedback, and
- generalization.

For many students, generalizing skills learned in class to other situations on campus, on the job, or in the home and community, is the most difficult part of social skills training. Thus, the teacher should periodically review the skills with the students and encourage them to use the skills outside class. By recruiting others on campus to help with reinforcement (such setting up a situation where the student must ask the media teacher for assistance in finding a reference, or asking the administrators to reinforce and reward the student when they observe him or her exhibiting appropriate social skills), the student can have additional instances to use and experience the value of using the skill he or she learned in class.

COMPETENCY 11.0 KNOWLEDGE OF PLANNING FOR INSTRUCTION

Skill 11.1 Explain how to utilize information provided by other professionals.

MENTAL HEALTH ASSESSMENTS

In categorizing mental health disorders many mental health professionals use the system of the Diagnostic and Statistical Manual, 4th edition, commonly referred to as DSM-IV. For children and adolescents, behavior disorders are coded and grouped into five broad categories called axes. The axes are as follows:

Axis I. Principal Psychiatric Diagnosis
Disruptive behavior disorders (e.g., 313.8I--oppositional defiant)
Anxiety disorders of childhood or adolescence
Eating disorders (e.g., pica)
Gender Identity disorder
Tic Disorders (e.g., Tourette's disorder)
Elimination disorders (e.g., enuresis)
Speech disorders such as cluttering or stuttering
Other disorders, including elective mutism

Axis II: Developmental Disorders
e.g., 317.00--Mild mental retardation
Includes mental retardation, pervasive developmental disorders, and academic, language, and motor skills disorders

Axis III: Physical Disorders (e.g., Allergies)

Axis IV. Psychosocial stressors (e.g., death or divorce in family)

Axis V: Highest level of adaptive intellectual and social functioning (on the Global Assessment of Functioning scale). Behaviors are rated on a scale of 1 to 90 in severity, with 1 being very severe, 60 as moderate, and minimal or absent of 90.

When interpreting mental health assessments, the teacher should be aware that diagnostic procedures usually take place in an office setting and may often rely on verbal reports (i.e., parents, teachers, self-report), rather than direct observation. Such reports may not be truly objective or accurate, depending on who is doing the reporting. Thus, different clinicians may not necessarily interpret the same information in the same way. Also, there is the issue of validity when one attempts to diagnostic constructs or internal processes, such as anxiety.

Anyone interpreting a mental health assessment should examine:

1. The manner in which the statement of the presenting problems was written. The more clearly the behavior is described, the less chance for error.
2. Types of assessment procedures and instruments used
3. Whether the proposed outcomes include a variety of follow-up activities and multidisciplinary planning.

BEHAVIORAL ASSESSMENTS

Behavioral assessments view the behavior as the problem, and searches for roots in some sort of biological, physical, or social stimulus.

The first phase involves the screening and identification process. Here the purpose is to determine if a problem exists. Things to consider in reading a behavioral assessment are:

- The description of the problems that led to the referral
- Settings and conditions under which the problem behavior occurs
- The types of instruments used in the screening, such as rating scales (standardized or not), teacher ratings, interviews, self-reports, or sociometric procedures,
- Who supplied the information for the ratings--parents, teacher, student

Following an examination of the behavioral assessment, the second part of the assessment interpretation involves the defining the problem and identifying the student's strengths and weaknesses, as well as ecological assessment to determine what contributes to the behavior. Once this step is done, the teacher can move on to pinpoint target behaviors and plan interventions.

Skill 11. 2 Demonstrate ability to analyze student data.

Analysis of student data requires the teacher to find the answers to these questions:

1. What type of behavior was being measured? The observer should describe the behavior in specific behavioral terms so that the reader will have no doubt about what does or does not constitute the behavior.

67

2. *What type of measurement strategy was used?* Meaningful data collection depends upon choosing the right measurement strategy for the target behavior. The four types of measurement strategies commonly used in behavioral analysis are:

- *Frequency* (rate)--how often a behavior occurs in a time interval (i.e., a student calling out in class or hitting other classmates). Frequency is also called tallying or event recording. Behaviors which are nondiscrete (without an observable beginning or end) are not suitable for this method.
- *Duration*--how long a behavior lasted (i.e., temper tantrums, time on task, thunbsucking). This method also must be used with discrete behaviors.
- *Latency*--length of time between the a stimulus and a targeted behavior (i.e., question and answer, request and compliance, prompt to begin work and the time the student actually begins the assignment). Latency also is used with discrete behaviors.
- *Intensity*--measures the frequency and duration of a behavior

3. *What type of recording procedure was used?* Knowing how the data was collected will enable the teacher to accurately analyze the behavior. Such recording procedures commonly used to establish baselines as well as determine effectiveness of behavioral interventions are:

- *Permanent products*--Student work as evidenced by numerical counts of correct answers, percent or rate of correct performances, trials to criterion)
- *Event recording*--for behaviors which are brief and discrete, with a definite beginning and end, such as call-outs, out-of-seat, or hitting.
- *Duration recording*--for behaviors which also have an easily observable beginning and end, such as time off task or out of seat.
- *Time Sampling, or Interval recording*-- Selecting an interval of a block of time to determine if the behavior is occurring during the sample time (i.e., 5 minutes out of an hour, or a sample every 5 minutes). This method is useful with nondiscrete behaviors such as playing, eating, or daydreaming, as well as with discrete behaviors. Interval recording is also useful for observing several students and one or more target behaviors.
- *Observation of more than one behavior or student*

4. *What measures have been taken to insure reliability?*--This involves the specificity and objectivity in describing the behavior. Pinpoint behaviors which are narrow in scope, and specifically defined with active verbs produce more observer reliability than behaviors that are vague. For example, "John is shy." is open to the observer's personal interpretation of shyness. "John does not initiate or maintain eye contact during a conversation with classmates" is more specific and less open to personal interpretation. If information on inter-rater reliability is included in the assessment, high percentages of agreement between the observers indicate high degrees or reliability.

Behavioral data may be reported statistically or visually with charts or graphs. An advantage of charts and graphs is the ability to see changes in behavior over a time interval. Data may be depicted in several ways:

♦ *Bar graphs* may be chosen to demonstrate group progress toward a goal, percents, and are usually easily understood.
♦ *Line graphs* are good for depicting cumulative progress, especially for positive behaviors, so that students can see increases in appropriate behavior.
♦ *Frequency polygons* may be used for rate, percents, or frequency data. They are noncumulative, and often used for making data-based decisions.
♦ *Progress charts and graphs* mark student progress toward objectives and mastery. Performance graphs show a change in a single task or behavior..

Skill 11.3   Select and write IEP goals and objectives.

IEP goals and objectives can address areas such as knowledge-based (academic), communication, interpersonal skills, vocational, and self-care. Goals and objectives need to be written based on the student's individual needs, not based on what is generally expected of students for a particular grade level. Computer programs have been developed to assist teachers in writing IEPs, but they should not be used to produce "cookie cutter" IEPS. Criterion-referenced evaluation materials are useful for formulating objectives and are preferred because they do not compare the student to other students.

A statement of the level of performance is written for each domain of the student's IEP. The determination of the level of performance may be derived from placement evaluation information (i.e., norm-referenced or criterion-referenced tests) or from informal assessments. The statement of performance should provide sufficient information to enable the teacher to formulate goals and objectives. For example, "Diane is below grade level in math" is vague and does not give the reader much information about what Diane can and cannot do. "Diane can add and subtract fractions with mixed numbers but cannot reduce or change fractions to mixed numbers." is a more accurate description of what the student can actually do.

For each target area on the IEP, an annual goal is written which should encompass the short-term goals and realistically describe what the student should be able to do at the end of the school year. A scope and sequence skills list is useful in selecting and writing annual goals. An annual goal may read: "Student will add and subtract fractions and mixed numbers with like and unlike denominators." At least 2 short-term objectives should be written for each annual goal. These objectives must be written in specific and measurable terms, such as "Helen will correctly divide two-syllable words."

Goals and objectives must also state *who is responsible* for assisting the student to reach the goal (EH teacher, speech/language teacher, the student himself), the *criterion for mastery* (the % accuracy needed, number of attempts, or number of words or problems given), the *schedule for evaluation* (when the goals and objectives will be examined to determine mastery), and *the date* they are or are not mastered.

Skill 11.4   Identify prerequisite skills using a given curriculum

Publishers of reading and content area textbooks and programs usually include a scope and sequence listing of skills for the program. The scope and sequence may describe the skill across grade levels or list the sequence of skills for the course of a single school year. The teacher can identify prerequisite skills for each objective in a scope and sequence using task analysis. For each objective, the teacher should be able to identify a condition, a criterion, and a terminal behavior. Starting with the terminal behavior (i.e., multiply a two-digit number by a one-digit number), the teacher works backward and lists each of the steps in order. These steps, or enabling behaviors, become the prerequisite skills for the task. Informal assessment can be used to determine which skills a student can perform, and instruction can begin with that step.

Skill 11.5   Correlate learning styles and skill levels with instructional strategies and materials.

Learning Styles refers to the ways that individuals learn best. Physical Settings, instructional arrangements, materials, techniques, and individual preferences all are factors in the teacher's choice of instructional strategies and materials. Information about the student's preference can be done through a direct interview or a Likert-style checklist where the student rates his preferences.

Physical Settings

A. Noise. Students vary in the degree of quiet that they need and the amount of background noise or talking that they can tolerate without getting distracted or frustrated.
B. Temperature and Lighting. Students also vary in their preference for lighter or darker areas of the room, tolerance for coolness or heat, and ability to see the chalkboard, screen, or other areas of the room.
C. Physical Factors. This refers to the student's needs for work space, and preference for type of work area, such as desk, table, or learning center.

Proximity factors such as closeness to other students, the teacher, or high traffic areas such as doorways or pencil sharpeners, may help the student to feel secure and stay on task, or may serve as distractions, depending on the individual.

Instructional Arrangements

Some students work well in large groups; others prefer small groups or one-to-one instruction with the teacher, aide, or volunteer. Instructional arrangements also involve peer tutoring situations with the student as tutor or tutee. The teacher also needs to consider how well the student works independently with seat work.

Instructional Techniques

Consideration of the following factors will affect the teacher's choice of instructional techniques, as well as selecting optimal times to schedule certain types of assignments. Some of these factors are listed below:

- How much time the student needs to complete work
- Time of day the student works best
- How student functions under timed conditions
- How much teacher demonstration and attention is needed for the task
- The student's willingness to approach new tasks
- Student's tendency to give up
- Student's frustration tolerance when faced with difficulty
- Student's preference for verbal or written instruction
- Number of prompts, cues, and attention needed for the student to maintain expected behavior.

Material and Textbook Preferences

Students vary in their ability to respond and learn with different techniques of lesson presentation. They likewise vary in their preference and ability to learn with different types of materials. Depending on the student's preference and success, the teacher can choose from among these types of instructional materials:

- Self-correcting materials
- Worksheets with or without visual cues
- Worksheets with a reduced number of items or lots of writing space
- Manipulative materials
- Flash cards, commercial or student-prepared

- Computers
- Commercial materials
- Teacher-made materials
- Games, board or card
- Student-made instructional materials

Learning Styles

Students also display preferences for certain learning styles and these differences also are factors in the teacher's choice of presentation and materials.

A) **Visual.** Students who are visual may enjoy working with and remember best from books, films, pictures, modeling, overheads, demonstration, and writing.

B) **Auditory.** Students who are auditory may enjoy working with and remember best from hearing records or tapes, auditory directions, listening to people, radio, read-aloud stories, and lectures.

C) **Tactile.** Indicators are drawing, tracing, manipulating, and working with materials such as clay or paints.

Kinesthetic. Indicators include learning through writing, experiments, operating machines such as typewriters and calculators, motor activities and games, and taking pictures.

Skill 11.6 Demonstrate the ability to organize student groups by learning styles and skill levels, incorporating the matching of instruction, strategies, and materials.

Five basic types of grouping arrangements are typically used in the classroom."

A. *Large-Group with Teacher.* Examples of appropriate activities include show and tell, discussions, watching plays or movies, brainstorming idea, and playing games. Science, social studies, and most other subjects except for reading and math, are taught in large groups.

The advantage of large-groups instruction is that it is time-efficient and prepares students for higher levels of secondary and postsedondary education settings. However, with large groups instruction cannot be not as easily tailored to high or low levels of students, who may become bored or frustrated. Mercer and Mercer recommend guidelines for effective large-group instruction:

* Keep instruction short, ranging from 5 to 15 minutes for first grade to 5 to 40 minutes for grades 8 to 12.
* Use questions to involve all students, use lecture-pause routines, and encourage activate participation among the lower performing students.
* Incorporate visual aids to promote understanding, and maintain a lively pace.
* Break up the presentation with change rate of talking, giving students a "stretch" break, varying voice volume, etc.
* Establish rules of conduct for large groups and praise students who follow the rules.

B. *Small Group Instruction*

Small group instruction usually includes 5 to 7 students and is recommended for teaching basic academic skills such as math facts or reading. This model is especially effective for students with learning problem. Composition of the groups should be flexible to accommodate different rates of progress through instruction. The advantages of teaching in small groups is that the teacher is better able to provide feedback, monitor student progress, and give more instruction, praise, and feedback. With small groups the teacher will need to make sure to provide a steady pace for the lesson, provide questions and activities that allow all to participate, and include lots of positive praise.

C. *One Student with Teacher*

One-to-one tutorial teaching can be used to provide extra assistance to individual students. Such tutoring may be scheduled at set times during the day or provided as the need arises. The tutoring model is typically found more in elementary and resource classrooms than secondary settings.

D. *Peer Tutoring*

In an effective peer tutoring arrangement, the teacher trains the peer tutors and matches them with students who need extra practice and assistance. In addition to academic skills, the arrangement can help both students work on social skills such as cooperation and self-esteem. Both students may be working on the same material or the tutee may be working to strengthen areas of weakness. The teacher determines the target goals, selects the material, sets up the guidelines, trains the student tutors in the rules and methods of the sessions, and monitors and evaluates the sessions.

E. *Cooperative Learning*

Cooperative learning differs from peer tutoring in that the students are grouped in teams or small groups and the methods are based on teamwork, individual accountability, and team reward. Individual students are responsible for their own learning and share of the work, as well as the group's success. As with peer tutoring, the goals, target skills, materials and guidelines are developed by the teacher. Teamwork skills may also need to be taught, too. By focusing on team goals, all members of the team are encouraged to help each other as well as improve their individual performance.

Skill 11.7 Exhibit knowledge of how to select and adapt instructional strategies as appropriate.

The choice of instructional strategy primarily depends upon the needs of the students. Information from the IEP and assessment reports can give the teacher information on what type of instructional modifications are recommended for a particular child. Interviews with the student as well as interest inventories can also help the teacher select instructional strategies that students identify as helping them learn best. Interest inventories can be teacher-made, commercial prepared, or on computer programs. From these the teacher can construct a class profile.

From the profile, the teacher would be able to determine learning styles--whether the students are visual, auditory, or kinesthetic. For a group of primarily visual learners, for example, a lecture would probably not be very effective unless it were accompanied by visual aids. Students also have preferences for certain types of materials over others, such as manipulative materials over worksheets.

The cognitive level of the students also will affect the type of strategy. Students who have trouble with abstract concepts will need hands-on, concrete instruction strategies to help them develop the foundation for understanding the abstract. An example of this would be using Cusinaire rods to develop knowledge of fractions.

Choice of instructional strategy also is influences by the type of task. Teaching a mnemonic device is effective to help a student remember the names of the planets in order, whereas an outline is more useful for reviewing a history chapter. Other factors influencing choice of strategy involve the frustration level, motivation and attitude toward certain tasks, need for supervision and assistance, ability to work independently or in a group, and variations in time needed to complete assignments.

Skill 11.8 Explain how to utilize activities designed for large group/small group/individual work.

Small group instruction is excellent for teaching basic skills such as math, reading, and writing. Therefore, it is often used for elementary grades. The groups should be as homogeneous as possible and flexible to allow students to move from group to group at their own rate. Motivation activities that are especially suited to small group work includes positive praise, descriptive praise, group praise, a fast pace, and enthusiasm from the teacher.

Content area subjects such as science and social studies are usually taught in large groups. The variety of individuals in a larger group is ideal for class discussions, cooperative learning, playing games, and brainstorming. However, the pace and scope of large-group instruction can become too slow or too fast for higher achievers and lower achievers. Therefore, instruction include a balance of higher-level and lower-level questions that involve all students in the lesson. Large group instruction should involve a lively pace and use plenty of visual aids such as diagrams, concept maps, and story maps to help students understand the relationships.

Individual tutoring and seatwork can be done for short periods of time daily to help students learn a new concept. These tutoring times can be done at scheduled times or spontaneously as the teacher observes a student having problems. Peer tutoring is effective with materials that the teacher has already given to the students, as long as the teacher has established the goals of the tutoring session, planned specific materials and academic skills to focus on, and trained the students who will act as tutors, and matched the student pairs appropriately.

Skill 11.9 Explain how to employ motivational strategies.

Before the teacher begins instruction, he or she should choose activities that are at the appropriate level of student difficulty, are meaningful and relevant. Teacher behaviors that motivate students include:

⇒ Maintain Success expectations through teaching goal setting, establishing connections between effort and outcome, and self-appraisal and reinforcement.

⇒ Have a supply of extrinsic incentives such as rewards, appropriate competition between students, and the value of the academic activities

⇒ Focus on the student Intrinsic motivation through adapting the tasks to student interests, providing opportunities for active response, including

75

variety of tasks, providing rapid feedback, incorporating games in the lesson, allowing students the opportunity to make choices, create, and interact with peers.

⇒ Stimulate students to learn by modeling positive expectations and attributions. Project enthusiasm and personalize abstract concepts. Students will be better motivated if they know what they will be learning about. The teacher should also model problem-solving and task related thinking so students can see how the process is done.

For adolescents, motivation strategies are usually aimed at getting the student actively involved in the learning process. Since the adolescent has the opportunity to get involved in a wider range of outside activities (job, car, being with friends), stimulating motivation may be the main focus even more than academics. Motivation may be done by through extrinsic reinforcers or intrinsic reinforcers. This is accomplished through allowing the student a degree of choice in what will be taught or how it will be done. The teacher will, if possible, obtain a commitment either through a verbal or a written contract between the student and the teacher. Adolescents also respond to regular feedback, especially if that feedback shows hat they are making progress.

Rewards for adolescents often include free time for listening to music, recreation, or games. They may like extra time for a break or exemption from a homework assignment. They may receive a reward at home for satisfactory performance at school. Other rewards include self-charting progress and tangible reinforcers. In summary, motivational activities may be used for goal setting, self-recording of academic progress, self-evaluation, and self-reinforcement.

Skill 11.10 Distinguish need for high/low level of activity.

Students may at first be unable to stick with a task for a long period. To develop time on task, break up the session into shorter ones. The time spent on task can be gradually lengthened. Complex tasks may be broken down into steps that increase gradually in complexity.

Highly preferred activities should be alternated with less preferred activities. This strategy is also known as "Grandma's Law" or the Premack Principle. The more difficult academics should be scheduled early in he day so the student can finish them and move on.

76

Skill 11.11   Explain how to combine semi-independent/independent practice.

The purpose of practice is to help the student move through the acquisition of learning a skill (initial learning) to maintenance (remembering how to do the skill) to generalization (applying the skill in new or different situations).

During guided, or semi-independent practice, the teacher should provide specific directions and model the procedure on the practice materials while the student follows along. Gradually the teacher prompts and modeling will fade out as the student becomes more proficient. Positive and corrective feedback should be applied by the teacher at this stage.

During independent practice, the teacher's role is to monitor the students and provide individual attention and modeling as necessary. The students should be encouraged to "think aloud" so the teacher can monitor what strategies and problem solving skills are being used to answer the questions. Again, positive and/or corrective feedback with praise should be used for achievement.

Skill 11.12   Distinguish need for high/low cognitive level questions.

Questions can be used to involve all students in the class discussions. The higher level questions should be asked of the high-ability students and less demanding ones to lower-ability students. Questions can be used to have students stretch their thinking and challenge them to extend what they have learned. Opening the lesson with a question can stimulate interest in the upcoming activity and get the students thinking about what will happen in the lesson. Throughout the lesson, teacher questions are usually one of these types:

- Lower level for recall or recognition or basic facts. (Who wrote <u>White Fang</u>?)

- Descriptive, or comparison questions are used for the acquisition of specific information and organization of information. (Compare the lifestyle of the Native Americans in Mexico before and after the arrival of the Spanish in the 1500s)

- Explanation questions and synthesis/summary questions, are used to interpret information and form conclusions. (How did the novels of Charles Dickens influence social reform in England?)

- Judgmental/Open-ended questions require one to apply divergent thinking and evaluate the quality or truth of a relationship or conclusion. (If farmers were not allowed to use any sort of pesticides on their crops, what effect would that have on food prices?)

Skill 11.13   Distinguish the need for teacher/peer directed instruction.

Teacher-directed instruction is used with students with learning problems because these students in many cases have deficiencies or "gaps" in their academic skills and because they may not have had opportunities to develop learning strategies.   They may have not have a chance to develop certain prerequisite skills necessary for understanding of basic concepts.

Teacher-directed instruction consists of presenting material in clear, step-by-step strategy and developing mastery at each step.   The teacher provides corrections for student process errors and gradually fades out teacher direction to independent work.   Opportunities to practice are given, as well as cumulative reviews.

Peer-directed instruction may take the form of peer tutoring or cooperative learning.   In peer tutoring, students work in pairs to provide more intensive practice in specific academic skills or additional practice in the content that the rest of the class is working on.   The material should be content that has already been presented in class, usually lower-level skills such as math facts or spelling words.   Tutors are trained in the tutoring and assessment procedure; students may take turns being tutor and tutee.

In cooperative learning, small groups of students work together to complete a task.   Students are held responsible for their share of the task and learning, as well as the success of the team.   Individuals must practice the skills and learn the content if their team is to be successful.

Skill 11.14   Specify a plan for the utilization of an aide/volunteer.

Teacher aides and volunteers can become an integral part of the classroom teaching process.   Teacher aides may be full- or part-time, depending on the budget and the program.   Generally, programs serving the more severely disturbed will have an aide that exclusively works with one teacher.   Otherwise, teachers will need to maximize the benefit of the time that the aide comes to the classroom.   Classroom duties may be categorized as follows:

Paperwork: Classroom aides can correct students' homework, seatwork, and tests.   They can observe and collect data on behavior, as well as chart student progress on graphs.   Aide can also prepare materials for tutoring and learning centers, such as flash cards and worksheets.   If the teacher needs to modify a textbook for a student, the aide can help with this task by tape recording or highlighting texts, key portions of texts. The aide can also be used for "housekeeping" duties such as making bulletin boards, photocopying, and filing.

Classroom Instruction. Classroom aides can help individual students with making up work after an absence, or tutor students who need extra practice with a difficult assignment. They can help conduct activities such as listening to students read, read aloud or tell stories to student groups, and help the teacher with hands-on activities.

Behavior and Classroom Management. The classroom aide should be thoroughly familiar with the teacher's behavior management system and implement it consistently. The classroom aide should be able to provide reinforcement as well as consequences, and the students should provide the same respect to the aide's direction as they would the teacher. The aide may assist with monitoring students who are in time-out or in a seclusion time-out room. However, classroom aides should not be used to implement physical intervention or transporting techniques without being appropriately trained in accordance with district policies and procedures.

Classroom Aides also can help with conflict resolution and play with the students during recreation activities, supervision on field trips, computer and board games, and arts and crafts with the students. For more severely disabled students, aides may assist students in personal and self-care. Aides are also role models who can listen when students need to talk.

Volunteers may offer their services for the specific purpose of working with students. If that is the case, volunteers may be used with those students who need extra practice and tutoring in content areas. They may also do such things are read to groups, observe and record behavioral data, or check papers.

Important points about classroom aides:
- Incorporate them into the classroom and behavior management system
- Train them to perform observation and recording tasks
- Integrate their strengths and areas of expertise into classroom teaching experiences
- Where volunteer or aide time is limited, prioritize things that need to be done
- Let the aide or volunteer know specifically the things the teacher expects of them

Skill 11.15   Show how to budget time for activities.

Schedule development depends upon the type of class (elementary or secondary) and the setting (regular classroom or resource room). There are, however, general rules of thumb that apply to both types and settings.

1. Allow time for transitions, planning, and setups.

2. Aim for maximum instructional time by pacing the instruction quickly and allotting time for practice of the new skills.

3. Proceed from short assignments to long ones, breaking up long lessons or complex tasks into short sessions or step-by-step instruction.

4. Follow a less preferred academic or activity with a highly preferred academic or activity.

5. In settings where students are working on individualized plans, do not schedule all the students at once in activities that require a great deal of teacher assistance. For example, have some students work on math or spelling while the teacher works with the students in reading, which usually requires more teacher involvement.

6. Break up a longer segment into several smaller segments with a variety of activities.

Special Considerations for Elementary Classrooms

1. Determine the amount of time that is needed for activities such as P.E., lunch, or recess.

2. Allow about 15-20 minutes each for opening and closing exercises. Spend this time for "housekeeping" activities such as collecting lunch money, going over the schedule, cleaning up, reviewing the day's activities, getting ready to go home.

3. Schedule academics for periods when the students are more alert and motivated, usually in the afternoon

4. Build in time for slower students to finish their work; others may work at learning centers or other activities of interest. Allowing extra time gives the teacher time to give more attention where it is needed, conduct assessments, or students to complete or correct work.

Special Considerations for Secondary Classes

Secondary school days are usually divided into five, six, or seven class periods of about 50 minutes, with time for homeroom and lunch. Students cannot stay behind and finish their work, since they have to leave for a different room. Resource room time should be scheduled so that the student does not miss academic instruction in his classroom or miss desirable nonacademic activities. In schools where ESE teachers also co-teach or work with students in the regular classroom, the regular teacher will have to coordinate lesson plans with those of the special education teacher. Consultation time will also have to budgeted into the schedule.

Homework

Mercer and Mercer recommend that homework should be planned at the instructional level of the student and incorporated into the learning process of the regular class work., The number and length of time needed will vary according to the age and grade level. Recommended times are:

- Primary grades--three 15 minute assignments per week.

- Grades 4 to 6--two to four 15- to 45-minute assignments per week.

- Grades 7 to 9--up to five 45- to 75-minute assignments per week.

- Grades 10 to 12--up to five 75- to 120-minute assignments per week

Skill 11.16 Specify lesson review and reteaching opportunities.

Each new lesson should begin with a daily review of the important facts, rules, and concepts of the previous lesson. The review may incorporate questions from the teacher, a brief quiz, checking homework, and feedback on homework. On the basis of the students' responses to the questions, the teacher can adjust the instruction of the lesson to go over areas that were not mastered or retained.

Reviews of the lesson can also be in the form of a synopsis and teacher questioning at the end of the lesson to see whether the students have learned the material. At the beginning of the next day, if the teacher sees that the students responded correctly at the end of the previous lesson, but not in the day-after review, they may need work on retention strategies.

Homework provides review opportunities for independent practice. Review should be done on a daily basis, with weekly and monthly cumulative reviews to provide information on retention of knowledge as well as provide opportunities to "overlearn" the materials.

Review and practice of skills can be done also in peer tutoring and cooperative learning arrangements, as well as individual student seatwork. Opportunities to reteach should be done when errors are observed. By immediately correcting the errors, the student is not inadvertently reinforced for the wrong process. Opportunities to reteach can also appear in student questions about present material that refer back to previous material.

Skill 11.17 Evaluate effectiveness of instruction.

Mastery of an instructional aim or goal is generally expressed in percentages, but may also be measured in terms of rate, or correct/incorrect responses per minute.

80% is usually the percent used for mastery of a concept. The teacher can use rate data from students who are making satisfactory progress and use their performances as aims. Another way is to obtain several scores on similar tasks and choose the median of the baseline scores as an aim, for example, in reading words per minute.

Charting data helps to illustrate student level of performance, the rate of change, variability of performance, and weekly performance. Ideally, analysis of the data will show a clear increase in the rate of correct responses and a decrease in incorrect responses. Chart analysis can also show if the student is starting to fall behind. If a student's progress is unsatisfactory for several days in a row, modifications in content or teaching strategy may need to be made for that student.

COMPETENCY 12. 0   KNOWLEDGE OF RECORD KEEPING

Skill 12.1   Identify essential elements of record keeping.

Elements of good record keeping are simplicity of use, good organization, durability, completeness, and regular updating. The system should be easy to use and understand so that others can help maintain the record keeping or interpret the results. The system should be well-organized to allow room for additions or changes without becoming messy or confusing. Before setting up the records, the teacher needs to make sure that all the report includes all the elements (i.e., student numbers, phone numbers, mastery dates, persons spoken to, objective numbers) before recording. Durability means that the records will hold up under long-term or frequent use. Finally, good record-keeping involves regular updating and commitment. If data entry is not done on a regular basis, it is easy to misplace or forget details, resulting in gaps of information. Missing information not only gives an incomplete picture of a student's progress, but may mean that a student could be delayed in receiving needed services. In due process cases, missing information may have legal implications.

All teachers are required to keep records of attendance and grades. Accuracy is essential, since these documents may be subpoenaed as evidence in legal matters. Lesson plans are also kept and should list (a) the objectives, (b) materials and texts used, (c) teacher activities, (d) student activities, and (e) evaluation criteria/methods. It is also important for the teacher to keep records of parent contacts for each student, listing the date, time, person spoken to, and brief summary of the conversation. This information is proof that the teacher has kept the parents informed of their child's behavior and/or progress, as well as any problems that are occurring.

Keeping records of classroom interventions is also important. Intervention logs for individual students provide proof of types of interventions for students who are being considered for placement in special programs, proof of programming interventions for students being considered for a change of placement, and important information about the effectiveness of different interventions with children. An intervention log should contain dates, brief description of the intervention used, length of time used, and results. Formal observations for target behaviors include charts and graphs for specific interventions, with baseline information, data on behavior during the intervention, data at the second baseline, and data after the reinstatement of the intervention. In programs where seclusion time-out is used, records must also be kept on the dates, times, duration, behaviors, and results of each seclusion time-out.

With regard to planning for instruction, two types of record keeping may be used: (a) a composite record for the entire class in a content area's objectives and skills, and (b) individual student record of mastery dates for objectives and skills in a content area. These records enable the teacher to determine areas of weaknesses for the entire class as well as pinpoint individual problem areas. By keeping accurate record charts, the teacher can plan for remediation or extra practice. The next two sections describe these types of records.

COMPOSITE RECORD KEEPING

A composite record is a system of recording student progress throughout a school year. The composite record can be used not only to document class progress, but also to group students for instruction. As students master objectives, they can be switched to different groups during the year. Elementary teachers will keep separate records for the different instructional areas; secondary teachers will maintain records for the content areas that they teach. Record forms may be available from the textbook publisher, or may be teacher-made. Computer programs may also be used for composite records.

- Composite records may be prepared in this manner:
- List instructional objectives in a sequential hierarchy.
- Write objectives in specific and measurable terms.
- List objectives in larger units than daily objectives (e.g., "Add fractions" is a larger unit than "Add fractions with like denominators."
- Organize objectives in steps that may be measured in short periods of time (i.e., a few days to a few weeks)

DAILY RECORDING

Daily record keeping is done for short-term objectives and can be organized like a table. The top part of the table includes the objectives for the time period and space for the teacher to record the date mastered. Student names would compose the rows of the table going down the sides of the page. Progress charts can also be prepared for individual students. For example, a chart can record number of correct and incorrect responses for spelling or math skills.

Tally sheets can be used to record performance of social skills objectives, such as out-of-seat behavior, raising hand, or volunteering responses to teacher questions. When the teacher uses this type of tally sheet, it is necessary to:
- Write the measurable short-term objective
- Determine and list the measurement that is being used (e.g., rate, percent, frequency
- Measurement schedule and method of assessment

LEARNING CENTER RECORDS

Learning centers should have a means of recording student progress at the enter. These could be checklists which the student completes and places in a work folder, a wall chart near the learning center for all the students to use, or a teacher checklist of activities the student is to complete. These records help the teacher to know what the student has been doing and what progress is being made.

2. Document student progress.

Report cards are probably the first thing that come to mind as documentation of a student's progress. The previous section discussed documentation of progress through daily and composite records of student mastery of curriculum objectives. Data gathered through tallies of nonacademic behavior can also be documented on charts and graphs. When sending home progress reports, it is important for the teacher to state and explain the measurement system being used so that the parents can understand the system Student progress can also be documented through other ways. Student folders with work samples (e.g., composition or spelling) can be kept so the student can see progress in the quality of work.

COMPETENCY 13.0   KNOWLEDGE AND USE OF CURRICULUM AND MATERIALS

Skill 13.1   Recognize curriculum standards in basic academic areas.

Effective curriculum design assists the student from teacher demonstration to independent practice. Components of curriculum design include
- quizzes or reviews ofd the previous lesson
- step-by-step presentations with multiple examples
- guided practice and feedback
- independent practice that requires the student to produce faster responses

The chosen curriculum should introduce information in a cumulative sequence and now introduce too much new information at a time.   Review of difficult material and practice to build retention. New vocabulary and symbols should be introduced one at a time, and the relationships of components to the whole should be stressed.   Students' background information should be recalled to connect new information to the old. Finally, teach strategies or algorithms first and then move on to more difficult tasks.

Course objectives may be obtained from the department head at the local school.   The ESE coordinator may have copies of objectives for functional courses or applied ESE courses. District program specialists also have lists of objectives for each course provided in the local school system. Additionally, publishers of textbooks will have scope and sequence lists in the teacher's manual.

Skill 13.2   Identify appropriate curriculum resources and materials.

General Characteristics

When choosing materials, the teacher should first consider the target population of the material and the major goals of the program materials. Cost compared with similar materials that teach the same skills, as well as durability and timeliness are factors in material selection. Material which is quickly out of date or does not withstand lots of use would not be a good choice. Field test data should be available to judge the program's effectiveness.

Teaching Factors

Objectives for the material should be listed, along with a scope and sequence. The skills should proceed from simple to complex and be presented in a logical order. Directions should be clear and concise. The teacher will want to examine the task levels (concrete, semi-concrete, or abstract?) as well as the organization of the material (units, chapters, and lessons). The teacher should look at the types of stimulus and response modalities used, as well as ways to asses entry-level in the curriculum. The teacher should also look for evidence of effective teaching procedures and the pace of the content.

Classroom Management Characteristics

The materials should provide a means of evaluation and data recording. The material should be judged on the basis of extent of teacher involvement, space and storage requirements, and time requirements. The materials should keep up student interest, and there should be reinforcement or suggestions for reinforcement. Students should be able to use the materials without disturbing others. The materials should be easy to set up or move, and be able to be used in flexible time limits. The teacher should see whether the student will be able to use the materials without the constant feedback or intervention of the teacher.

Skill 13.3 Select teacher-made and commercial materials to match learning needs

The first step in the process would be to make informal assessments of the areas the student is having trouble with as well as learning styles and preferences. If the materials come with a scope and sequence or summary of objectives and skills, the teacher can select those portions which match the student's needs. Since commercial materials are not always written with special needs students in mind, there are things that teachers can do to make these materials easier to use.

1. Review the materials and add advance organizers, cues, prompts, and feedback steps as necessary to make sure that the lesson contains the elements of explicit teaching procedures.

2. Tape record directions, stories, or specific lessons so that the student can listen and play them back as needed.

3. Clarify written directions by underlining key phrases or direction words. If the directions are too lengthy or wordy, simplify and rewrite them.

4. For students who are anxious about seeing what appears to be too much work, tear out individual pages or present portions of the assignment.

5. Students who are distracted by the visual stimuli of a full page can cover sections that they are not working on at the moment.]

6. Change the response directions to underlining, multiple choice, marking, or sorting if the student has a problem with handwriting. Give extra space for writing answers if needed.

7. Develop reading guides, outlines of lectures, glossary for content area materials that do not come with one, and graphic organizers.

8. Develop a method of marking a place in consumable materials.

9. Use tape recorders, computer-assisted instruction, overhead projectors with transparencies, Language Masters, and self-correcting materials.

COMPETENCY 14.0 PROFICIENCY IN BEHAVIOR MANAGEMENT

Skill 14.1 Identify and explain assertive discipline.

Assertive discipline, developed by Canter and Canter, is an approach to classroom control that allows the teacher to constructively deal with misbehavior and maintain a supportive environment for the students. The assumptions behind assertive discipline are:

* Behavior is a choice
* Consequences for not following rules are natural and logical, not a series of threats or punishments.
* Positive reinforcement occurs for desired behavior
* The focus is on the behavior and the situation, not the student's character

The assertive discipline plan should be developed as soon as the teacher meets the students. The students can become involved in developing and discussing the needs for the rules. Rules should be limited to 4 to 6 basic classroom rules which are simple to remember and positively stated (e.g., "Raise hand to speak" instead of "Don't talk without permission."

1. *Recognize and remove roadblocks to assertive discipline.* Replace negative expectations with positives, and set reasonable limits for the children.

2. *Practice an assertive response style.* That is, clearly state teacher expectations and expect the students to comply with them.

3. *Set limits.* Take into consideration the students' behavioral needs, the teacher's expectations, and set limits for behavior. Decide what you will do when the rules are broken or complied with.

4. *Follow through promptly with the consequences when students break the rules.* However, the students should clearly know in advance what to expect when a rule is broken. Conversely, also follow through with the promised rewards for compliance and good behavior. This reinforces the concept that individuals choose their behavior and that there are consequences for their behavior.

5. *Devise a system of positive consequences.* Positive consequences do not have to always be food or treats. However, rewards should not be promised if it is not possible to deliver them. The result is a more positive classroom.

1. **One technique that has proven especially effective in reducing self-stimulation and repetitive movements in autistic or severely retarded children is:**

   A. Shaping

   B. Overcorrection

   C. Fading

   D. Response cost

2. **In math class, Mary talked out without raising her hand. Her teacher gave her a warning and asked her to state the rule for being recognized to speak. However, Mary was soon talking out again and lost a point from her daily point sheet. This is an example of:**

   A. Shaping

   B. Overcorrection

   C. Fading

   D. Response cost

3. **Which body language would not likely be interpreted as a sign of defensiveness, aggression, or hostility?**

   A. Pointing

   B. Direct eye contact

   C. Hands on hips

   D. Arms crossed

4. **The minimum number of IEP meetings required per year is:**

   A. As many as necessary

   B. One

   C. Two

   D. Three

5. **Satisfaction of the LRE requirement means that**

   A. The school is providing the best services it can offer there

   B. The school is providing the best services the district has to offer

   C. The student is being educated with the fewest special education services necessary

   D. The student is being educated in the least restrictive setting that meets his or her educational needs

6. **A review of a student's eligibility for an exceptional student program must be done:**

   A. At least once every 3 years

   B. At least once a year

   C. Only if a major change occurs in academic or behavioral performance

   D. When a student transfers to a new school

7. **Crisis intervention methods are above all concerned with:**

   A. Safety and self-being of the staff and students

   B. Stopping the inappropriate behavior

   C. Preventing the behavior from occurring again

   D. The student learning that otbursts are inappropriate

8. **Ricky, a third grade student, runs out of the classroom and onto the roof of the school. He paces around the roof, looks around to see who is watching, and laughs at the people standing on the ground. He appears to be in control of his behavior. What should the teacher do?**

   A. Go back inside and leave him up there until he decides he is ready to come down

   B. Climb up to get Ricky so he doesn't fall off and get hurt

   C. Notify the crisis teacher and arrange to have someone monitor Ricky

   D. Call the police

9. **Judy, a fourth grader, often is looking around the room or out the window. She does not disturb anyone, but has to ask for directions to be repeated and does not finish her work. Her teacher decides to reinforce Judy when she is on task. This would be an example of which method of reinforcement?**

   A. Fading

   B. DRO

   C. DRI

   D. Shaping

10. **An appropriate time out for a ten-year-old would be:**

    A. Ten minutes

    B. Twenty minutes

    C. No more than one-half hour

    D. What ever time it takes for the disruptive behavior to stop

11. During the science lesson Rudy makes remarks from time to time, but his classmates are not attending to them. The teacher reinforces the students who are raising their hand to speak, but ignores Rudy. The teacher reinforces Rudy when he raises his hand. This technique is an example of:

A. Fading

B. Response Cost

C. Extinction

D. Differential Reinforcement of Incompatible behavior

12. Mike was caught marking up the walls of the bathroom with graffiti. His consequence was to clean up all the walls of the bathroom. This type of overcorrection would be:

A. Response Cost

B. Restitution

C. Positive Practice

D. Negative Practice

13. Which of these would probably not be a result of implementing an extinction strategy?

A. Maladaptive behavior gets worse before it gets better

B. Maladaptive behavior stops, then starts up again for a brief time.

C. Aggression may occur for a brief period following implementation of extinction

D. The length of time and patience involved to implement the strategy might tempt the teacher to give up.

14. Witholding or removing a stimulus that reinforces a maladaptive behavior is:

A. Extinction

B. Overcorrection

C. Punishment

D. Reinforcing an incompatible behavior

15. Which of these would not be used to strengthen a desired behavior?

A. Contingency contracting

B. Tokens

C. Chaining

D. Overcorrection

16. If the arrangement in a fixed-ratio schedule of reinforcement is 3, when will the student receive the reinforcer?

A. After every third correct response

B. After every third correct response in a row

C. After the third correct response in the time interval of the behavior sample

D. After the third correct response even if the undesired behavior occurs in between correct response

17. Wesley is having trouble ignoring distractions. At first you have him seated at a carrel which is located in a corner of the room. He does well, so you eventually move him out of the carrel for increasing portions of the day. Eventually he is able to sit in a seat with the rest of his classmates. This is an example of:

A. Shaping

B. Extinction

C. Fading

D. Chaining

18. Laura is beginning to raise her hand first instead of talking out. An effective schedule of reinforcement would be:

A. Continuous

B. Variable

C. Intermittent

D. Fixed

19. As Laura continues to raise her hand to speak, the teacher would want to change to this schedule of reinforcement in order to wean her from the reinforcement:

A. Continuous

B. Variable

C. Intermittent

D. Fixed

20. Hen Laura has demonstrated that she has mastered the goal of raising her hand to speak, reinforcement during the maintenance phase should be:

A. Continuous

B. Variable

C. Intermittent

D. Fixed

21. As integral part of ecological interventions are consequences that:

A. Are natual and logical

B. Include extinction and overcorrection

C. Are immediate and consistent

D. Involve fading and shaping

22. Examples of behaviors that are appropriate to be measured for their duration included all EXCEPT:

A. Thumb-sucking

B. Hitting

C. Temper tantrums

D. Maintaining eye contact

23. Examples of behaviors that are appropriate to be monitored by measuring frequency include all EXCEPT:

A. Teasing

B. Talking out

C. Being on time to class

D. Daydreaming

24. Criteria for choosing behaviors to measure by frequency include all but those that:

A. Have an observable beginning

B. Last a long time

C. Last a short time

D. Occur often

25. Criteria for choosing behaviors to measure by duration include all but those that:

A. Last a short time

B. Last a long time

C. Have no readily observable beginning or end

D. Don't happen often

26. Data on quiet behaviors (e.g., nail biting or daydreaming) are best measured using a:

A. Interval or time sample

B. Continuous sample

C. Variable sample

D. Fixed-ratio sample

27. Mr. Jones wants to design an intervention for reducing Jason's sarcastic remarks. He wants to find out who or what is reinforcing Jason's remarks, so he records data on Jason's behavior as well as the attending behavior of his peers. This is an example of collecting data on

A. Reciprocal behaviors

B. Multiple behaviors for single subjects

C. Single behaviors for multiple subjects

D. Qualitative data on Jason

28. Ms. Beekman has a class of students who frequently talk out. She wishes to begin interventions with the students who are talking out the most. She monitors the talking behavior of the entire class for 1 minute samples every half hour. This is an example of collecting data on:

A. Multiple behaviors for single subjects

B. Reciprocal behaviors

C. Single behaviors for multiple subjects

D. Continuous behaviors for fixed intervals

29. Mark got a B on his social studies test. Mr. Wilner praised him for his good grade but he replies, "I was lucky this time. It must have been an easy test." Mark's statement is an example of:

A. External locus of control

B. Internal locus of control

C. Rationalization of his performance

D. Modesty

30. Mr. Smith is on a field trip with a group of high school EH students. On the way they stop at a fast-food restaurant for lunch, and Warren and Raul get into a disagreement. After some heated words, Warren stalks out of the restaurant and refuses to return to the group. He leaves the parking lot, continues walking away from the group, and ignores Mr. Smith's directions to come back. What would be the best course of action for Mr. Smith?

A. Leave the group with the class aide and follow Warren to try to talk him into coming back.

B. Wait a little while and see if Warren cools off and returns

C. Telephone the school and let the crisis teacher notify the police in accordance with school policy

D. Call the police himself

31. Which is the least effective of reinforces in programs for mildly to moderately handicapped learners?

A. Tokens

B. Social

C. Food

D. Activity

32. Tyrone likes to throw paper toward the trash can instead of getting up to throw it away. After several attempts of positive interventions, Tyrone has to serve a detention and continue to throw balls of paper at the trash can for the entire detention period. This would be an example of:

A. Negative practice

B. Overcorrection

C. Extinction

D. Response cost

33. A student may have great difficulty in meeting a target goal if the teacher has not first considered:

A. If the student has external or internal locus of control

B. If the student is motivated to attain the goal

C. If the student has the essential prerequisite skills to perform the goal

D. If the student has had previous success or failure meeting the goal in other classes

34. The Premack Principle of increasing the performance of a less-preferred activity by immediately following it with a highly-preferred activity is the basis of:

A. Response cost

B. Token systems

C. Contingency contracting

D. Self-recording management

35. Mr. Brown finds that his chosen consequence does not seem to be having the desired effect of reducing the target misbehavior. Which of these would LEAST LIKELY account for Mr. Brown's lack of success with the consequence?

A. The consequence was aversive in Mr. Brown's opinion but not the students'

B. The students were not developmentally ready to understand the connection between the behavior and the consequence

C. Mr. Brown was inconsistent in applying the consequence

D. The intervention had not previously been shown to be effective in studies

36. Teaching techniques that stimulate active participation and understanding in the mathematics class include all but which of the following?

A. Having students copy computation facts for a set number of times

B. Asking students to find the error in an algorithm

C. Giving immediate feedback to students

D. Having students chart their progress.

37. Justin, a second grader, is reinforced if he is on task at the end of each 10-minute block of time that the teacher observes him. This is an example of what type of reinforcement schedult?

A. Continuous

B. Fixed-interval

C. Fixed-ratio

D. Variable ratio

38. Addressing a student's maladaptive behavior right away with a "time out" should be reserved for situations where:

A. The student has engaged in the behavior continuously throughout the day

B. Harm might come to the student or others

C. Lesser interventions have not been effective

D. The student displayed the behavior the day before

39. At the beginning of the school year, Annette had a problem with being late to class. Her teacher reinforced her each time she was in her seat when the bell rang. In October, her teacher decided to reward her every other day when she was not tardy to class. The reinforcement schedule appropriate for making the transition to maintenance phase would be:

A. Continuous

B. Fixed interval

C. Variable Ratio

D. Fixed Ratio

40. By November, Annette's teacher is satisfied with her record of being on time and decides to change the schedule of reinforcement. The best type of reinforcement schedule for maintenance of behavior is:

A. Continuous

B. Fixed interval

C. Variable Ratio

D. Fixed-ratio

41. Which of these groups is not comprehensively covered by IDEA?

A. Gifted and talented

B. Mentally retarded

C. Specific learning disabilities

D. Speech and language impaired

42. Organizing ideas by use of a web or outline is an example of which writing activity.

A. Revision

B. Drafting

C. Prewriting

D. Final draft

43. When a teacher is choosing behaviors to modify, the issue of social validity must be considered. Social validity refers to:

A. The need for the behavior to be performed in public

B. Whether the new behavior will be considered significant by those who deal with the child

C. Whether there will be opportunities to practice the new behavior in public

D. Society's standards of behavior

44. Dena, a second grader, is a messy eater who leaves her lunch area messy as well. Dena's teacher models correct use of eating utensils, and napkins for her. As Dena approximates the target behavior of eating neatly and leaving her area clean, she receives praise and a token. Finally Dena reaches her target behavior goal and redeems her tokens. Dena's teacher used strategy of:

A. Chaining

B. Extinction

C. Overcorrection

D. Shaping

45. Educators who advocate educating all children in their neighborhood classrooms and schools, propose the end of labeling and segregation of special needs students in special classes, and call for the delivery of special supports and services directly in the classroom may be said to support the:

A. Full Service Model

B. Regular Education Initiative

C. Full Inclusion Model

D. Mainstream Model

46. In Ellis's ABC model, maladaptive behavior in response to a situation results from:

A. Antecedent events

B. Stimulus events

C. Thinking abuot the consequences

D. Irrational beliefs about the event

47. Section 504 differs from the scope of IDEA because its main focus is on:

A. Prohibition of discrimination on basis of disability

B. A basis for additional support services and accommodations in a special education setting

C. Procedural rights and safeguards for the individual

D. Federal funding for educational services

48. Public Law 99-457 amended the IDEA to make provisions for:

A. Education services for "uneducable" children

B. Educational services for children in jail settings

C. Special education benefits for children birth to five years

D. Educational services for medically fragile children

49. A holistic approach to stress management should include all of the following EXCEPT

A. Teaching a variety of coping methods

B. Cognitive modification of feelings

C. Teaching the flight or fight response

D. Cognitive modification of behaviors

50. Marisol has been mainstreamed into a ninth grade language arts class. Although her behavior is satisfactory and she likes the class, Marisol's reading level is about two years below grade level. The class has been assigned to read "Great Expectations" and write a report. What intervention would be LEAST successful in helping Marisol co0mplete this assignment?

A. Having Marisol listen to a taped recording while following the story in the regular text.

B. Giving her a modified version of the story

C. Telling her to choose a different book that she can read

D. Showing a film to the entire class and comparing and contrasting it to the book

51. Fractions may be thought of in each of these ways EXCEPT:

A. Part of a whole

B. Part of a parent set

C. Ratio

D. An exponent

52. Many special education students may have trouble with the skills necessary to be successful in algebra and geometry for all but one of these reasons:

A. Prior instruction focused on computation rather than understanding

B. Unwillingness to problem solve

C. Lack of instruction in prerequisite skills

D. Large amount of new vocabulary

53. Which of these process is NOT directly related to the meaningful development of number in young children:

A. Describing

B. Classifying

C. Grouping

D. Ordering

54. **Mr. Ward wants to assess Jennifer's problem-solving skills in mathematics. Which question would not address her use of strategies?**

A. Does Jennifer check for mistakes in computation?

B. Does Jennifer use trial and error to solve problems?

C. Does Jennifer have an alternative strategy if the first one fails?

D. Does Jennifer become easily frustrated if she doesn't immediately get an answer?

55. **Ryan is working on a report about dogs. He uses scissors and tape to cut and rearrange sections and paragraphs, then photocopies the paper so he can continue writing. Ryan is in which stage of the writing process?**

A. Final Draft

B. Prewriting

C. Revision

D. Drafting

56. **Talking into a tape recorder is an example of which writing activity?**

A. Prewriting

B. Drafting

C. Final Draft

D. Revision

57. **Publishing a class newsletter, looking through catalogues and filling out order form, and playing the role of secretaries and executives are activities designed to teach:**

A. Expressive writing

B. Transactional writing

C. Poetic writing

D. Creative writing

58. **Under the provisions of IDEA, the student is entitle to all of these EXCEPT:**

A. Placement in the best environment

B. Placement in the least restrictive environment

C. Provision of educational needs at no cost

D. Provision of individualized, appropriate educational program

59. Teacher modeling, student-teacher dialogues, and peer interactions are part of which teaching technique designed to provide support during the initial phases of instruction?

A. Reciprocal teaching

B. Scaffolding

C. Peer tutoring

D. Cooperative learning

60. Modeling of a behavior by an adult who verbalizes the thinking process, overt self-instruction, and covert self-instruction are components of:

A. Rational-Emotive Therapy

B. Reality Therapy

C. Cognitive Behavior Modification

D. Reciprocal Teaching

61. Standards of accuracty for a student's spelling should be based on the student's:

A. Grade level spelling list

B. Present reading book level

C. Level of spelling development

D. Performance on an informal assessment

62. Which of these techniques is least effective in helping children correct spellingproblems:

A. The teacher models the correct spelling in a context

B. Student sees the incorrect and the correct spelling together in order to visualize the correct spelling

C. Positve reinforcement as the child tests the rules and tries to approximate the correct spelling

D. Copying the correct word 5 times

63. The single most important activity for eventual reading success of young children is:

A. Giving them books

B. Watching animated stories

C. Reading aloud to them

D. Talking about pictures in books

64. Skilled readers use all but which one of these knowledge sources to construct meanings beyond the literal text:

A. Text knowledge

B. Syntactic knowledge

C. Morphological knowledge

D. Semantic knowledge

65. The cooperative nature of Glasser's Reality Therapy, in which problem-solving approach is used to correct misbehavior, is best signified by:

A. Minimal punishment

B. It's similar approach to methods that teach students how to deal with academic mistakes

C. Students' promises to use the alternative behavior plan to help them reach their goals

D. Procedure sheets used during conflict situations

66. Diaphragmatic breathing, progressive relaxation training, and exercises are examples of which type of stress coping skills?

A. Rational-emotive

B. Cognitive-psychological

C. Somatic-physiological

D. Stress innoculation

67. The stress that we experience when we win a race or accomplish a difficult task is called:

A. Stressor

B. Stresses

C. Eustress

D. Distress

68. Jane is so intimidated by a classmate's teasing that she breaks down in tears and cannot stand up for herself. The feelings she is experiencing is:

A. Stressors

B. Stresses

C. Eustress

D. Distress

69. The movement toward serving as many children with disabilities as possible in the regular classroom with supports and services is known as:

A. Full Service Model

B. Regular Education Initiative

C. Full Inclusion Model

D. Mainstream Model

70. Which of the following is NOT a feature of effective classroom rules:

A. They are about 4 to 6 in number

B. They are negatively stated

C. Consequences for infractions are consistent and immediate

D. The can be tailored to individual classroom goals and teaching styles

71. A suggested amount of time for large-group instruction lesson for a sixth or seventh grade group would be:

A. 5 to 40 minutes

B. 5 to 20 minutes

C. 5 to 30 minutes

D. 5 to 15 minutes

72. Sam is working to earn half an hour of basketball time with his favorite PE teacher. At the end of each half hour Sam marks his point sheet with an X if he reached his goal of no call-outs. When he has received 25 marks, he will receive his basketball free time. This behavior management strategy is an example of:

A. Self-recording

B. Self evaluation

C. Self-reinforcement

D. Self-regulation

73. Mark has been working on his target goal of completing his mathematics classwork. Each day he records on a scale of 0 to 3 how well he has done his work and his teacher provides feedback. This self-management technique is an example of:

A. Self-recording

B. Self-reinforcement

C. Self-regulation

D. Self-evaluation

74. When Barbara reached her target goal, she chose her reinforcer and softly said to herself, "I worked hard and I deserve this reward." This self-management technique is an example of:

A. Self-reinforcement

B. Self-recording

C. Self-regulation

D. Self-evaluation

75. Grading should be based on all of the following EXCEPT

A. Clearly defined mastery of course objectives

B. A variety of evaluation methods

C. Performance of the student in relation to other students

D. Assigning points for activities and basing grades on a point total.

76. The following words describe an IEP objective EXCEPT:

A. Specific

B. Observable

C. Measurable

D. Criterion-referenced

77. Teacher feedback, task completion, and a sense of pride over mastery or accomplishment of a skill are examples of:

A. Extrinsic reinforcers

B. Behavior modifiers

C. Intrinsic reinforcers

D. Positive feedback

78. Social approval, token reinforcers, and rewards such as pencils or stickers are examples of:

A. Extrinsic reinforcers

B. Behavior modifiers

C. Intrinsic reinforcers

D. Positive feedback reinforcers

79. Aggression, escape, and avoidance are unpleasant side effects which can be avoided by using:

A. Time out

B. Response cost

C. Overcorrection

D. Negative practice

80. Josie forgot that it was school picture day and did not dress up for the pictures. In the media center, Josie notices some girls in the line waiting to have their pictures taken. They appear to be looking over at her and whispering. Josie feels certain that they are making fun of the way her hair and clothes look and gets so upset that she leaves the line and hides out in the bathroom. Josie did not think to ask when the makeup day for pictures would be. According to Ellis's ABC Model, Josie's source of stress is:

A. Her forgetting to dress appropriately for picture day

B. The girls in the library who appear to be whispering about her

C. Her belief that they are making fun of her appearance

D. The girls' insensitive behavior

81. Token systems are popular for all of these advantages EXCEPT:

A. The number needed for rewards may be adjusted as needed

B. Rewards are easy to maintain

C. They are effective for students who generally do not respond to social reinforcers

D. Tokens reinforce the relationship of desirable behavior and reinforcement

82. Which would not be an advantage of using a criterion-referenced test?

A. Information about an individual's ability level is too specific for the purposes of the assessment.

B. It can pinpoint exact areas of weaknesses and strengths

C. You can design them yourself

D. You do not get comparative information

83. Which is NOT an example of a standard score?

A. T Score

B. Z Score

C. Standard deviation

D. Stanine

84. The most direct method of obtaining assessment data and perhaps the most objective is:

A. Testing

B. Self-recording

C. Observation

D. Experimenting

85. **The basic tools necessary to observe and record behavior include all BUT:**

A. Cameras

B. Timers

C. Counters

D. Graphs or charts

86. **Which of these characteristics is NOT included in the P. L. 94-142 definition of emotional disturbance:**

A. General pervasive mood of unhappiness or depression

B. Social maladjustment manifested in a number of settings

C. Tendency to develop physical symptoms, pains, or fear associated with school or personal problems

D. Inability to learn which is not attributed to intellectual, sensory, or health factors

87. **Of the various factors that contribute to delinquency and antisocial behavior, which has been found to be the weakest?**

A. Criminal behavior and/or alcoholism in the father

B. Lax mother and punishing father

C. Socioeconomic disadvantage

D. Long history of broken home or marital discord among parents

88. **Poor moral development, lack of empathy, and behavioral excesses such as aggression are the most obvious characteristics of which behavioral disorder?**

A. Autism

B. ADD-H

C. Conduct disorder

D. Pervasive developmental disorder

89. **School refusal, obsessive-compulsive disorders, psychosis, and seperation anxiety are also frequently accompanied by:**

A. Conduct disorder

B. ADD-H

C. Depression

D. Autism

90. Signs of depression do not typically include:

A. hyperactivity

B. Changes in sleep patterns

C. Recurring thoughts of death or suicide

D. Significant changes in weight or appetite

91. Children who are characterized by impulsivity generally:

A. Do not feel sorry for their actions

B. Blame others for their actions

C. Do not weigh alternatives before acting

D. Do not outgrow their problem

92. Which of these is listed as only a minor scale on the Behavior Problem Checklist?

A. Motor Excess

B. Conduct Disorder

C. Socialized Aggression

D. Anxiety-Withdrawal

93. The extent that a test measures what it claims to measure is called:

A. Reliability

B. Validity

C. Factor Analysis

D. Chi Square

94. Which is not a goal of collaborative consultation?

A. Prevent learning and behavior problems with mainstreamed students

B. Coordinate the instructional programs between mainstream and ESE classes

C. Facilitate solutions to learning and behavior problems

D. Function as an ESE service model

95. An important goal of collaborative consultation is:

A. Mainstream as many ESE students as possible

B. Guidance on how to handle ESE students from the ESE teacher

C. Mutual empowerment of both the mainstream and the ESE teacher

D. Document progress of mainstreamed students

96. **Knowledge of evaluation strategies, program interventions, and types of data are examples of which variable for a successful consultation program?**

A. People

B. Process

C. Procedural implementation

D. Academic preparation

97. **Skills as an administrator, and background in client, consulter, and consultation skills are examples of which variable in a successful consultation program?**

A. People

B. Process

C. Procedural implementation

D. Academic preparation

98. **The ability to identify problems, generate solutions, and knowledge of theoretical perspectives of consultation are examples of which variable in a successful consultation program?**

A. People

B. Process

C. Procedural implementation

D. Academic preparation

99. **A serious hindrance to successful mainstreaming is:**

A. Lack of adapted materials

B. Lack of funding

C. Lack of communication among teachers

D. Lack of support from administration

100. **Which of the following statements was not offered as a rationale for the REI?**

A. Special education students are not usually identified until their learning problems have become severe

B. Lack of funding will mean that support for the special needs children will not be available in the regular classroom

C. Putting children in segregated special education placements is stigmatizing

D. There are students with learning or behavior problems who do not meet special education requirements but who still need special services

101. **The key to success for the exceptional student placed in a regular classroom is:**

   A. Access to the special aids and materials

   B. Support from the ESE teacher

   C. Modifications in the curriculum

   D. The mainstream teacher's belief that the student will profit from the placement

102. **Lack of regular follow-up, difficulty in transporting materials, and lack of consistent support for students who need more assistance are disadvantages of which type of service model?**

   A. Regular Classroom

   B. Consultant with Regular Teacher

   C. Itinerant

   D. Resource Room

103. **Ability to supply specific instructional materials, programs, and methods, and to influence environmental learning variables are advantages of which service model for exceptional students?**

   Regular Classroom

   Consultant Teacher

   Itinerant Teacher

   Resource Room

104. **An emphasis on instructional remediation and individualized instruction in problem areas, and a focus on mainstreaming students are characteristics of which model of service delivery?**

   A. Regular Classroom

   B. Consultant Teacher

   C. Itinerant Teacher

   D. Resource Room

105. **Which of these would not be considered a valid attempt to contact a parent for an IEP meeting?**

   A. Telephone

   B. Copy of correspondence

   C. Message left on an answering machine

   D. Record of home visits

106. **A best practice for evaluation student performance and progress on IEPs is:**

   A. Formal assessment

   B. Curriculum based assessment

   C. Criterion-based assessment

   D. Norm-referenced evaluation

107. **Guidelines for an Individualized Family Service Plan (IFSP) would be described in which legislation?**

A. PL 94-142

B. PL 99-457

C. PL 101-476

D. ADA

108. **In a positive classroom environment, errors are viewed as:**

A. Symptoms of deficiencies

B. Lack of attention or ability

C. A natural part of the learning process

D. The result of going too fast

109. **Recess, attending school social or sporting events, and eating lunch with peers are examples of:**

A. Privileges

B. Allowances

C. Rights

D. Entitlements

110. **Free time, shopping at the school store, and candy are examples of:**

A. Privileges

B. Allowances

C. Rights

D. Entitlements

111. **Eating lunch, access to a bathroom, and privacy are examples of:**

A. Privileges

B. Allowances

C. Rights

D. Entitlements

112. **Cheryl is a 15-year old student receiving educational services in a full-time EH classroom. The date for her IEP review will take place two months before her 16th birthday. According to the requirements of IDEA, what must ADDITIONALLY be included in this review?**

A. Graduation plan

B. Individualized transition plan

C. Individualized Family Service Plan

D. Transportation planning

113. Hector is a 10th grader in a program for the severely emotionally handicapped. After a classmate taunted him about his mother, Hector threw a desk at the other boy and attacked him. As crisis intervention team attempted to break up the fight, one teacher hurt his knee. The other boy received a concussion. Hector now faces disciplinary measures. How long can he be suspended without the suspension constituting a "change of placement"?

A. 5 days

B. 10 days

C. 10 + 30 days

D. 60 days

114. The concept that a handicapped student cannot be expelled for misconduct which is a manifestation of the handicap itself is not limited to students which was labeled "seriously emotionally disturbed:. Which reason does NOT explain this concept?

A. Emphasis on individualized evaluation

B. Consideration of the problems and needs of handicapped students

C. Right to a free and appropriate public education

D. Putting these students out of school will just leave them on the streets to commit crimes

115. An effective classroom behavior management plan includes all but which of the following?

A. Transition procedures for changing activities

B. Clear consequences for rule infractions

C. Concise teacher expectations for student behavior

D. Copies of lesson plans

116. Statements like "Darrien is lazy." Are not helpful in describing his behavior for all but which of these reasons?

   A. There is no way to determine if any change occurs from the information given.

   B. The student and not the behavior becomes labeled.

   C. Darrien's behavior will manifest itself clearly enough without any written description.

   D. Constructs are open to various interpretations among the people who are asked to define them.

117. Marcie often is not in her seat when the bell rings. She may be found at the pencil sharpener, throwing paper away, or fumbling through her notebook. Which of these descriptions of her behavior can be described as a "pinpoint"?

   A. Is tardy a lot

   B. Is out of seat

   C. Is not in seat when late bell rings

   D. Is disorganized

118. When choosing behaviors for change, the teacher should ask if there is any evidence that the behavior is presently or potentially harmful to the student or others. This is an example of which test?

   A. Fair-Pair

   B. "Stranger" Test

   C. Premack Principle

   D. "So-What?" Test

119. Ms. Taylor takes her students to a special gymnastics presentation that the P.E. coach has arranged in the gym. She has a rule against talk-outs and reminds the students that they will lose 5 points on their daily point sheet for talking out. The students get a chance to perform some of the simple stunts. They all easily go through the movements except for Sam, who is known as the class klutz. Sam does not give up, and finally completes the stunts. His classmates cheer him on with comments like "Way to go!". Their teacher, however, reminds them that they broke the no talking rule and will lose the points. What mistake was made here?

A. The students forgot the no-talking rule.

B. The teacher considered talk-outs to be maladaptive in all school settings

C. The other students could have distracted Sam with talk-outs and caused him to get hurt

D. The teacher should have let the P. E. coach handle the discipline in the gym

120. Which of the following should be avoided when writing objectives for social behavior?

A. Nonspecific adverbs

B. Behaviors stated as verbs

C. Criteria for acceptable performance

D. Conditions where the behavior is expected to be performed

121. Criteria for choosing behaviors that are in the most need of change involve all but the following:

A. Observations across settings to rule out certain interventions

B. Pinpointing the behavior that is the poorest fit in the child's environment

C. The teacher's concern about that is the most important behavior to target

D. Analysis of the environmental reinforcers

122. Ms. Wright is planning an analysis of Audrey's out-of-seat behavior. Her initial data would be called:

A. Pre-referral phase

B. Intervention phase

C. Baseline phase

D. Observation phase

123. To reinforce Audrey each time she is on-task and in her seat, Ms. Wright decides to deliver specific praise and stickers which Audrey may collect and redeem for a reward. The data collected during the time Ms. Wright is using this intervention is called:

A. Referral phase

B. Intervention phase

C. Baseline phase

D. Observation pahse

124. Indirect requests and attempts to influence or control others through one's use of language is an example of:

A. Morphology

B. Syntax

C. Pragmatics

D. Semantics

125. Kenny, a fourth grader, has trouble comprehending analogies, using comparative, spatial, and temporal words, and multiple meanings. Language interventions for Kenny would focus on:

A. Morphology

B. Syntax

C. Pragmatics

D. Semantics

126. Celia, who is in first grade, asked, "Where my ball?" She also has trouble with passive sentences. Language interventions for Celia would target:

A. Morphology

B. Syntax

C. Pragmatics

D. Semantics

127. Scott is in middle school, but still says statements like " I gotted new high-tops yesterday." And "I saw three mans in the front office." Language interventions for Scott would target:

A. Morphology

B. Syntax

C. Pragmatics

D. Semantics

128. Which is not indicative of a handwriting problem?

A. Errors persisting over time

B. Little improvement on simple handwriting tasks

C. Fatigue after writing for a short time

D. Occasional letter reversals, word omissions, and poor spacing

129. All of these are effective in teaching written expression EXCEPT:

A. Exposure to various styles and direct instruction in those styles

B. Immediate feedback from the teacher with all mistakes clearly marked

C. Goal setting and peer evaluation of written products according to a set criteria

D. Incorporating writing with other academic subjects

130. Mr. Menedez is assessing his students' written expression. Which of these is not a component of written expression?

A. Vocabulary

B. Morphology

C. Content

D. Sentence Structure

131. Ms. Tolbert is teaching spelling to her students. The approach stresses phoneme-grapheme relationships within parts of words. Spelling rules, generalizations, and patterns are taught. A typical spelling list for her third graders might include light, bright, night, fright, and slight. Which approach is Ms. Tolbert using?

A. Rule-based Instruction

B. Fernald Method

C. Gillingham Method

D. Test-Study-Test

132. At the beginning of the year, Mr. Johnson wants to gain an understanding of his class's social structure in order to help him assess social skills and related problems. The technique that would best help Mr. Johnson accomplish this is:

A. Personal interviews with each student

B. Parent rating form

C. Sociometric techniques

D. Self-reports

133. In assessing a group's social structure, asking a student to listing the classmates whom he or she would choose to be his or her best friends, preferred play partners, and preferred work partners is an example of:

A. Peer nomination

B. Peer rating

C. Peer assessment

D. Sociogram

134. Naming classmates who fit certain behavioral descriptions such as smart, disruptive, or quiet, is an example of which type of sociometric assessment?

A. Peer nomination

B. Peer rating

C. Peer assessment

D. Sociogram

135. Mr. Johnson asks his students to score each of their classmates in areas such as who they would prefer to play with and work with. A likert-type scale with nonbehavioral criteria is used. This is an example of:

A. Peer nomination

B. Peer rating

C. Peer assessment

D. Sociogram

136. Which of these explanations would not likely account for the lack of a clear definition of behavior disorders?

A. Problems with measurement

B. Cultural and/or social influences and views of what is acceptable

C. The numerous types of manifestations of behavior disorders

D. Differing theories that use their own terminology and definitions

137. Ryan is 3, and her temper tantrums last for an hour. Bryan is 8, and he does not stay on task for more than 10 minutes without teacher prompts. These behaviors differ from normal children in terms of their:

A. Rate

B. Topography

C. Duration

D. Magnitude

138. All children cry, hit, fight, and play alone at different times. Children with behavior disorders will perform these behaviors at a higher than normal:

A. Rate

B. Topography

C. Duration

D. Magnitude

139. The exhibition of two or more types of problem behaviors across different areas of functioning is known as:

A. Multiple maladaptive behaviors

B. Clustering

C. Social maladjustment

D. Conduct disorder

140. Children with behavior disorders often do not exhibit stimulus control. This means that they have not learned:

A. The right things to do

B. Where and when certain behaviors are appropriate

C. Right from wrong

D. Listening skills

141. Social withdrawal, anxiety, depression, shyness, and guilt are indicative of:

A. Conduct disorder

B. Personality disorders

C. Immaturity

D. Socialized aggression

142. Short attention span, daydreaming, clumsiness, and preference for younger playmates are associated with:

A. Conduct disorder

B. Personality disorders

C. Immaturity

D. Socialized aggression

143. Truancy, gang membership, and feeling of pride in belonging to a delinquent subculture are indicative of:

A. Conduct disorder

B. Personality disorders

C. Immaturity

D. Socialized aggression

144. Temper tantrums, disruption of disobedience, and bossiness are associated with:

A. Conduct disorder

B. Personality disorders

C. Immaturity

D. Socialized aggression

145. Which of these is not true for most children with behavior disorders?

A. Many score in the "slow learner" or " mildly retarded" rang on IQ test.

B. They are frequently behind their classmates in terms of academic achievement.

C. They are bright, but bored with there surroundings.

D. A large amount of time is spent in nonproductive, nonacademic behaviors.

146. Ecolalia, repetitive stereotyped actions, and a severe disorder of thinking and communication are indicative of:

A. Psychosis

B. Schizophrenia

C. Autism

D. Paranoia

147. Teaching children functional skills that will be useful in their home life and neighborhoods is the basis of:

A. Curriculum-based instruction

B. Community based instruction

C. Transition planning

D. Functional curriculum

148. Disabilities caused by fetal alcohol syndrome are many times higher for which ethnic group?

A. Native Americans

B. Asian Americans

C. Hispanic Americans

D. African Americans

149. Which of these would be the least effective measure of behavioral disorders?

A. Projective test

B. Ecological assessment

C. Standardized test

D. Psychodynamic analysis

150. Which behavioral disorder is difficult to diagnose in children because the symptoms are manifested quite differently than in adults?

A. Anorexia

B. Schizophrenia

C. Paranoia

D. Depression

ANSWER KEY

1.	B	45. C	89. C	133.	A
2.	D	46. D	90. A	134.	B
3.	B	47. A	91. C	135.	C
4.	B	48. C	92. A	136.	C
5.	D	49. C	93. B	137.	C
6.	A	50. C	94. D	138.	A
7.	A	51. D	95. C	139.	B
8.	C	52. A	96. B	140.	B
9.	C	53. C	97. A	141.	B
10.	A	54. A	98. C	142.	C
11.	C	55. C	99. C	143.	D
12.	C	56. A	100. B	144.	A
13.	B	57. B	101. D	145.	C
14.	A	58. A	102. C	146.	C
15.	D	59. B	103. B	147.	B
16.	B	60. C	104. D	148.	A
17.	A	61. C	105. C	149.	C
18.	A	62. D	106. B	150.	D
19.	D	63. C	107. B		
20.	B	64. C	108. C		
21.	A	65. C	109. D		
22.	B	66. C	110. A		
23.	D	67. C	111. C		
24.	B	68. D	112. B		
25.	A	69. C	113. B		
26.	A	70. B	114. D		
27.	A	71. B	115. D		
28.	C	72. A	116. C		
29.	A	73. D	117. C		
30.	C	74. A	118. D		
31.	C	75. C	119. D		
32.	A	76. D	120. A		
33.	C	77. C	121. C		
34.	C	78. A	122. C		
35.	D	79. B	123. B		
36.	A	80. C	124. C		
37.	B	81. B	125. D		
38.	B	82. D	126. B		
39.	B	83. C	127. A		
40.	C	84. C	128. D		
41.	A	85. A	129. B		
42.	C	86. B	130. B		
43.	B	87. C	131. B		
44.	D	88. C	132. C		

"Mrs. Hammond, I'd know you anywhere from little Billy's portrait of you."

"Are we there yet?"